Grade 3

Pearson Scott Foresman

Leveled Reader
Teaching Guide

Glenview, Illinois • Boston, Massachusetts • Chandler, Arizona • Upper Saddle River, New Jersey

ISBN: 13: 978-0-328-48442-3
ISBN: 10:   0-328-48442-3
10 V016 15 14 13

CC1

Table of Contents

LEVELED READER TITLE	Instruction	Comprehension Practice	Vocabulary Practice
Camping with Aunt Julie	12–13	14	15
Let's Make a Trade!	16–17	18	19
Ice Fishing in the Arctic	20–21	22	23
The Shopping Trip	24–25	26	27
The Market Adventure	28–29	30	31
These Birds Can't Fly!	32–33	34	35
Iguana Takes a Ride	36–37	38	39
The Last Minute	40–41	42	43
Our Garden	44–45	46	47
Bills and Beaks	48–49	50	51
In the Fields	52–53	54	55
The Thunder and Lightning Men	56–57	58	59
Meet the Stars	60–61	62	63
What a Day!	64–65	66	67
Desert Life	68–69	70	71
A Trip	72–73	74	75
Measuring the Earth	76–77	78	79
Fun with Hobbies and Science!	80–81	82	83

Graphic Organizers

Introduction

Scott Foresman *Reading Street* provides more than 750 leveled readers that help children become better readers and build a lifelong love of reading. The *Reading Street* leveled readers are engaging texts that help children practice critical reading skills and strategies. They also provide opportunities to build vocabulary, understand concepts, and develop reading fluency.

The leveled readers were developed to be age-appropriate and appealing to children at each grade level. The leveled readers consist of engaging texts in a variety of genres, including fantasy, folk tales, realistic fiction, historical fiction, and narrative and expository nonfiction. To better address real-life reading skills that children will encounter in testing situations and beyond, a higher percentage of nonfiction texts is provided at each grade.

USING THE LEVELED READERS

You can use the leveled readers to meet the diverse needs of your children. Consider using the readers to

- practice critical skills and strategies
- build fluency
- build vocabulary and concepts
- build background for the main selections in the student book
- provide a variety of reading experiences, e.g., shared, group, individual, take-home, readers' theater

GUIDED READING APPROACH

The *Reading Street* leveled readers are leveled according to Guided Reading criteria by experts trained in Guided Reading. The Guided Reading levels increase in difficulty within a grade level and across grade levels. In addition to leveling according to Guided Reading criteria, the instruction provided in the *Leveled Reader Teaching Guide* is compatible with Guided Reading instruction. An instructional routine is provided for each leveled reader. This routine is most effective when working with individual children or small groups.

MANAGING THE CLASSROOM

When using the leveled readers with individuals or small groups, you'll want to keep the other children engaged in meaningful, independent learning tasks. Establishing independent practice stations throughout the classroom and child routines for these stations can help you manage the rest of the class while you work with individuals or small groups. Practice stations can include listening, phonics, vocabulary, independent reading, and cross-curricular activities. For classroom management, create a work board that lists the stations and which children should be at each station. Provide instructions at each station that detail the tasks to be accomplished. Update the board and alert children when they should rotate to a new station. For additional support for managing your classroom, see the *Reading Street* Practice Stations' *Classroom Management Handbook*.

USING THE LEVELED READER TEACHING GUIDE

The *Leveled Reader Teaching Guide* provides an instruction plan for each leveled reader based on the same instructional routine.

INTRODUCE THE BOOK The Introduction includes suggestions for creating interest in the text by discussing the title and author, building background, and previewing the book and its features.

READ THE BOOK Before students begin reading the book, have them set purposes for reading and discuss how they can use the reading strategy as they read. Determine how you want students in a particular group to read the text, softly or silently, to a specific point or the entire text. Then use the Comprehension Questions to provide support as needed and to assess comprehension.

REVISIT THE BOOK The Reader Response questions provide opportunities for students to demonstrate their understanding of the text, the target comprehension skill, and vocabulary. The Response Options require students to revisit the text to respond to what they've read and to move beyond the text to explore related content.

SKILL WORK The Skill Work box provides instruction and practice for the target skill and strategy and selection vocabulary. Instruction for an alternate comprehension skill allows teachers to provide additional skill instruction and practice for students.

USING THE GRAPHIC ORGANIZERS

Graphic organizers in blackline-master format can be found on pages 132–152. These can be used as overhead transparencies or as student worksheets.

ASSESSING PERFORMANCE

Use the assessment forms that begin on page 6 to make notes about your students' reading skills, use of reading strategies, and general reading behaviors.

MEASURE FLUENT READING (pp. 6–7) Provides directions for measuring a student's fluency, based on words correct per minute (wcpm), and reading accuracy using a running record.

OBSERVATION CHECKLIST (p. 8) Allows you to note the regularity with which students demonstrate their understanding and use of reading skills and strategies.

STUDENT SELF-ASSESSMENT (p. 9) Helps students identify their own areas of strength and areas where they need further work. This form (About My Reading) encourages them to list steps they can take to become better readers and to set goals as readers. Suggest that students share their self-assessment notes with their families so that family members can work with them more effectively to practice their reading skills and strategies at home.

READING STRATEGY ASSESSMENT (p. 10) Provides criteria for evaluating each student's proficiency as a strategic reader.

PROGRESS REPORT (p. 11) Provides a means to track a student's book-reading progress over a period of time by noting the level at which a student reads and his or her accuracy at that level. Reading the chart from left to right gives you a visual model of how quickly a student is making the transition from one level to the next. Share these reports with parents or guardians to help them see how their child's reading is progressing.

Measure Fluent Reading

Taking a Running Record

A running record is an assessment of a student's oral reading accuracy and oral reading fluency. Reading accuracy is based on the number of words read correctly. Reading fluency is based on the reading rate (the number of words correct per minute) and the degree to which a student reads with a "natural flow."

How to Measure Reading Accuracy

1. Choose a grade-level text of about 80 to 120 words that is unfamiliar to the student.
2. Make a copy of the text for yourself. Make a copy for the student or have the student read aloud from a book.
3. Give the student the text and have the student read aloud. (You may wish to record the student's reading for later evaluation.)
4. On your copy of the text, mark any miscues or errors the student makes while reading. See the running record sample on page 7, which shows how to identify and mark miscues.
5. Count the total number of words in the text and the total number of errors made by the student. Note: If a student makes the same error more than once, such as mispronouncing the same word multiple times, count it as one error. Self-corrections do not count as actual errors. Use the following formula to calculate the percentage score, or accuracy rate:

$$\frac{\text{Total Number of Words} - \text{Total Number of Errors}}{\text{Total Number of Words}} \times 100 = \text{percentage score}$$

Interpreting the Results

- A student who reads **95–100%** of the words correctly is reading at an **independent level** and may need more challenging text.
- A student who reads **90–94%** of the words correctly is reading at an **instructional level** and will likely benefit from guided instruction.
- A student who reads **89%** or fewer of the words correctly is reading at a **frustrational level** and may benefit most from targeted instruction with lower-level texts and intervention.

How to Measure Reading Rate (WCPM)

1. Follow Steps 1–3 above.
2. Note the exact times when the student begins and finishes reading.
3. Use the following formula to calculate the number of words correct per minute (WCPM):

$$\frac{\text{Total Number of Words Read Correctly}}{\text{Total Number of Seconds}} \times 60 = \text{words correct per minute}$$

Interpreting the Results

By the end of the year, a third-grader should be reading approximately 110–120 WCPM.

Running Record Sample

Running Record Sample

Dana had recently begun ✓✓✓✓ **4**
volunteering at the animal rescue ✓✓✓✓✓ **9**
shelter where her mom worked as a ✓✓✓✓✓✓✓ **16**
veterinarian. The shelter was (just) across **22**
the bay from their house. **27**

Dana was learning many different ✓✓✓✓✓ H **32**
jobs at the shelter. She fed the dogs ✓✓✓✓✓✓✓ **40**
and cleaned their cages. She played ✓✓✓✓✓✓ **46**
catch with the dogs in the shelter's ✓✓✓✓✓✓✓ **53**
backyard. Dana's favorite job, however, ✓✓ /jōb/ ✓ **58**
was introducing people to the dogs ✓✓✓✓✓✓ **64**
waiting for adoption. Whenever a dog ✓✓✓✓✓✓ **70**
found a new home, Dana was especially ✓✓✓✓✓ (sc) **77**
pleased! ✓ **78**

The road to the shelter crossed over ✓✓✓✓✓✓ **85**
the bay. Dana looked for boats in the ✓✓✓ the ✓✓✓✓ **93**
channel, but there were none. Dana's ✓✓✓✓✓ ^ **99**
mom turned on the radio to listen to ✓✓✓✓✓✓ hear ✓ **107**
the news as they drove. The weather ✓✓✓✓✓✓✓ **114**
reporter announced that a blizzard ✓✓✓✓ **119**
might hit some parts of the state. ✓✓✓✓✓✓ **126**

Notations

Accurate Reading
The student reads a word correctly.

Omission
The student omits words or word parts.

Hesitation
The student hesitates over a word, and the teacher provides the word. Wait several seconds before telling the student what the word is.

Mispronunciation/Misreading
The student pronounces or reads a word incorrectly.

Self-correction
The student reads a word incorrectly but then corrects the error. Do not count self-corrections as actual errors. However, noting self-corrections will help you identify words the student finds difficult.

Insertion
The student inserts words or parts of words that are not in the text.

Substitution
The student substitutes words or parts of words for the words in the text.

Running Record Results
Total Number of Words: **126**
Number of Errors: **5**

Reading Time: **64 seconds**

▶ **Reading Accuracy**
$\frac{126 - 5}{126}$ x 100 = 96.032 = 96%

Accuracy Percentage Score: **96%**

▶ **Reading Rate—WCPM**
$\frac{121}{64}$ x 60 = 113.44 = 113 words correct per minute

Reading Rate: **113 WCPM**

Observation Checklist

Student's Name _____ Date _____

Behaviors Observed	Always (Proficient)	Usually (Fluent)	Sometimes (Developing)	Rarely (Novice)
Reading Strategies and Skills				
Uses prior knowledge and preview to understand what book is about				
Makes predictions and checks them while reading				
Uses context clues to figure out meanings of new words				
Uses phonics and syllabication to decode words				
Self-corrects while reading				
Reads at an appropriate reading rate				
Reads with appropriate intonation and stress				
Uses fix-up strategies				
Identifies story elements: character, setting, plot, theme				
Summarizes plot or main ideas accurately				
Uses target comprehension skill to understand the text better				
Responds thoughtfully about the text				

Reading Behaviors and Attitudes				
Enjoys listening to stories				
Chooses reading as a free-time activity				
Reads with sustained interest and attention				
Participates in discussion about books				

General Comments

About My Reading

Name _____ Date _____

1. **Compared with earlier in the year, I am enjoying reading**

   ☐ more   ☐ less   ☐ about the same

2. **When I read now, I understand**

   ☐ more than I used to   ☐ about the same as I used to

3. **One thing that has helped me with my reading is**

   _____

   _____

   _____

4. **One thing that could make me a better reader is**

   _____

   _____

   _____

5. **Here is one selection or book that I really enjoyed reading:**

   _____

   _____

6. **Here are some reasons why I liked it:**

   _____

   _____

   _____

   _____

   _____

   _____

Reading Strategy Assessment

Student _____ Date _____

Teacher _____

		Proficient	Developing	Emerging	Not showing trait
Building Background Comments:	Previews	☐	☐	☐	☐
	Asks questions	☐	☐	☐	☐
	Predicts	☐	☐	☐	☐
	Activates prior knowledge	☐	☐	☐	☐
	Sets own purposes for reading	☐	☐	☐	☐
	Other:	☐	☐	☐	☐
Comprehension Comments:	Retells/summarizes	☐	☐	☐	☐
	Questions, evaluates ideas	☐	☐	☐	☐
	Relates to self/other texts	☐	☐	☐	☐
	Paraphrases	☐	☐	☐	☐
	Rereads/reads ahead for meaning	☐	☐	☐	☐
	Visualizes	☐	☐	☐	☐
	Uses decoding strategies	☐	☐	☐	☐
	Uses vocabulary strategies	☐	☐	☐	☐
	Understands key ideas of a text	☐	☐	☐	☐
	Other:	☐	☐	☐	☐
Fluency Comments:	Adjusts reading rate	☐	☐	☐	☐
	Reads for accuracy	☐	☐	☐	☐
	Uses expression	☐	☐	☐	☐
	Other:	☐	☐	☐	☐
Connections Comments:	Relates text to self	☐	☐	☐	☐
	Relates text to text	☐	☐	☐	☐
	Relates text to world	☐	☐	☐	☐
	Other:	☐	☐	☐	☐
Self-Assessment Comments:	Is aware of: Strengths	☐	☐	☐	☐
	Needs	☐	☐	☐	☐
	Improvement/achievement	☐	☐	☐	☐
	Sets and implements learning goals	☐	☐	☐	☐
	Maintains logs, records, portfolio	☐	☐	☐	☐
	Works with others	☐	☐	☐	☐
	Shares ideas and materials	☐	☐	☐	☐
	Other:	☐	☐	☐	☐

Progress Report

Student's Name _____

At the top of the chart, record the book title, its grade/unit/week (for example, 1.2.3), and the student's accuracy percentage. See page 6 for measuring fluency, calculating accuracy and reading rates. At the bottom of the chart, record the date you took the running record. In the middle of the chart, make an X in the box across from the level of the student's reading—frustrational level (below 89% accuracy), instructional level (90–94% accuracy), or independent level (95–100% accuracy). Record the reading rate (WCPM) in the next row.

Book Title						
Grade/Unit/Week						
Reading Accuracy Percentage						
LEVEL Frustrational (89% or below)						
Instructional (90–94%)						
Independent (95% or above)						
Reading Rate (WCPM)						
Date						

Camping with Aunt Julie

SUMMARY In this fictional story, a young boy goes on a camping trip in the desert with his aunt. This gives students information about different settings and shows how characters might act in a new setting.

LESSON VOCABULARY

bat	battery
blew	fuel
plug	term
vision	

INTRODUCE THE BOOK

INTRODUCE THE TITLE AND AUTHOR Discuss with students the title and author of *Camping with Aunt Julie*. Have students look at the cover art. Ask: What is the boy doing? What do you think this story will be about?

BUILD BACKGROUND Ask students whether they have ever gone camping or to a desert. Ask students to discuss how camping might be different from other ways of vacationing. Talk about how camping in a desert might be different from camping in other locations.

PREVIEW/TAKE A PICTURE WALK As students preview the book, encourage them to look closely at the illustrations and ask what information about the story these illustrations provide. Point out the expressions on the characters' faces, and ask students how this helps them understand what might be going on in the story.

READ THE BOOK

SET PURPOSE Have students set a purpose for reading *Camping with Aunt Julie*. Invite them to ask questions about the cover illustration and title, such as, "What would it be like to camp in the desert at night?" Students' curiosity about these topics should guide their purpose.

STRATEGY SUPPORT: PRIOR KNOWLEDGE Remind students that *prior knowledge* is what they already know about a subject. Prior knowledge might be gathered from their reading or personal experiences. Explain that connecting prior knowledge to text can help students understand what they read. Invite students to discuss camping trips and activities they have done.

COMPREHENSION QUESTIONS

PAGE 3 Based on the information presented about Aunt Julie, what do you think she is like? *(Aunt Julie is adventurous. She enjoys hiking in the mountains, doesn't need the comforts of home, and loves to travel.)*

PAGE 6 Why do you think that Scott's parents didn't object to the suggestion that he travel with Aunt Julie? *(Possible response: They were happy for him to have the opportunity to travel and might have thought that it would be a good learning experience for him.)*

PAGES 8–9 What does Scott think the trip will be like at first? What does he soon realize about the camping trip? *(Scott thought there would be a soft bed, television, and running water. At the mention of a tent, Scott realizes that he is going to be roughing it without the comforts of home.)*

PAGE 12 What happened when the bat flew over Scott's head? *(The bat scared Scott into helping put the tent up, for shelter.)*

REVISIT THE BOOK

READER RESPONSE

1. Possible responses: traveler, camper, happy, adventurous
2. Possible responses: Many nocturnal animals, such as bats, mice, and lizards, live in the desert. Scott might be frightened by these animals and fear sleeping in a tent in the desert.
3. *term;* the length of time that something lasts; Possible sentence: The President's term of office is four years.
4. Answers will vary but should include a reason the student would prefer to either camp out or stay in a hotel while traveling in the desert.

EXTEND UNDERSTANDING As students read the story, ask them to pay close attention to what the desert looks like in each of the illustrations. Discuss how the illustrations help tell the story.

RESPONSE OPTIONS

WRITING Ask students to write about other ways they or their family may have traveled. Perhaps they've camped out, stayed in a hotel, flown on an airplane, or sailed on a boat.

SCIENCE CONNECTION

Suggest that students find out more about how desert animals live. Provide a selection of books and magazines about desert animals. Have students choose an animal and create a poster that gives information about that animal.

Skill Work

TEACH/REVIEW VOCABULARY

Read aloud the vocabulary words. Ask students about words they may already know and explain words that are not familiar. Ask students what other meanings they might think of for the words *term* and *vision.*

ELL Find pictures of items commonly used for camping, such as tent, backpack, fire, and lantern. Help English language learners identify and label these items. Say the word as you label the item, and ask students to repeat the word.

TARGET SKILL AND STRATEGY

CHARACTER AND SETTING Remind students that the *character* is the person or animal that is doing the action of the story, and the *setting* is the time and place of the story. Explain that what a person does can show what kind of person he or she is. For example, if a person goes camping, we can imagine that that person enjoys nature. Encourage students to record details that show what Scott is like. Remind students that the *setting* can also influence how a character acts and that, as they read, they should make notes about the *setting* and about how the character acts in it.

PRIOR KNOWLEDGDE Tell students that thinking about what they already know about a topic can help them understand what they read. Suggest that if students use *prior knowledge,* they will be able to make better generalizations about the facts in the text. As they read, have them note at least one instance where they activate prior knowledge to help them understand the text.

ADDITIONAL SKILL INSTRUCTION

THEME Without using the word *theme,* remind students that many stories include one big idea, or lesson, about how people should act. Discuss the lessons in familiar stories such as *The Tortoise and the Hare* (slow and steady wins the race). Ask students how that big idea provides a lesson about how people should behave.

Character and Setting

- **Character** is the person or animal that is doing the action of the story.
- **Setting** is the time and place of the story.

Directions What kind of person is Aunt Julie in the story *Camping with Aunt Julie?* Read the details below, and then tell how those details describe the kind of person Aunt Julie is.

1. Aunt Julie returns from her travels and shares photos and with Scott. This shows she is

_____.

2. Aunt Julie invites Scott to join her on her camping trip to the desert. This shows she is

_____.

3. Aunt Julie drives up in a van full of camping things. This shows she is

_____.

4. Imagine you are on a camping trip in the desert. What would you do and why? How would set up camp and spend the evening in the desert? Write a short paragraph about your experience.

_____

_____

_____

_____

_____

_____

_____

_____

_____

Vocabulary

Directions Choose the word from the box that best completes each sentence. Write the word on the line. Two words are used more than once.

Check the Words You Know

___bat	___battery	___blew	___fuel
___plug	___term	___vision	

1. Dad _____ on the flame to get the campfire started.

2. The flashlight needed a _____ in order for it to work.

3. Wood, small sticks, and leaves were the perfect _____ for the campfire.

4. The CD player would not work without a _____ or _____.

5. My new glasses improve my _____, and I can see better.

6. The school _____ is sixteen weeks long.

7. The _____ flew over the desert at night.

8. The wind _____ through the trees.

Directions Select four vocabulary words and write a sentence for each one.

9. _____

_____

10. _____

_____

11. _____

_____

12. _____

_____

Let's Make a Trade!

SUMMARY This book explains the benefits and the fun of bartering as an alternative to using money. It gives a brief history of how bartering began and how coins and paper money came into use. The book encourages students to try bartering.

LESSON VOCABULARY

carpenter	carpetmaker
knowledge	marketplace
merchant	plenty
straying	thread

INTRODUCE THE BOOK

INTRODUCE THE TITLE AND AUTHOR Discuss with students the title and the author of *Let's Make a Trade!* Based on the title and the cover illustration, ask students to describe what they imagine this book will be about.

BUILD BACKGROUND Ask: Have you ever traded something of yours for something that belonged to someone else? That's bartering. Discuss what other kinds of bartering students may have done and how they decided what something might be worth.

PREVIEW/USE TEXT FEATURES Have students look at the illustrations and read the captions. Suggest that students consider what extra information these elements provide about bartering.

READ THE BOOK

SET PURPOSE Have students set a purpose for reading *Let's Make a Trade!* Students' interest in acquiring new things without using money may guide this purpose. They might also be interested in the history of bartering. Suggest that students think about how goods can be obtained through trade instead of with money.

STRATEGY SUPPORT: SUMMARIZE As students read about bartering, prompt them to identify and write down the most important idea from each page. After reading, direct them to write a summary paragraph, using their notes as a guide. Invite volunteers to share their summaries with the class.

COMPREHENSION QUESTIONS

PAGES 3 What other things besides goods can be bartered? (*knowledge and skill*)

PAGE 9 What is a bartering plan? (*a list that details what skills or items you have to offer and what skills or items you need*)

PAGES 10–11 How did bartering help the radio station? (*The radio station got office space in exchange for running free ads.*)

PAGES 12–13 After reading about the sequence of events during "Bartering Day," what do you think the sequence of events for any trade should be? (*One person selects an item he or she no longer wants or needs. He or she displays the item for trade, and another person looks at it. Both traders can barter, bargain, trade, or decide to keep their item.*)

REVISIT THE BOOK

READER RESPONSE

1. Students brought items from home; students displayed their items; students decided what to barter for; some students bartered.
2. The theater gave the radio station its unused office space, and the radio station gave the theater free advertising in return.
3. *stray*; Possible sentence: Don't let the puppy stray too far.
4. Possible responses: One dad could barter his knowledge of how to start a small business. The other dad could barter his ability to do carpentry.

EXTEND UNDERSTANDING Suggest that students look at the diagram on pages 8–9. Diagrams are visual aids that can help you better understand the text. As students look at the diagram, ask them to discuss how the pictures help them understand what is being bartered. Draw students' attention to the arrows on pages 8–9 and ask how these arrows explain bartering more clearly.

RESPONSE OPTIONS

WRITING Have students write scripts for commercials that advertise something they are willing to barter. Invite students to perform their commercials for the class.

SOCIAL STUDIES CONNECTION

Time For SOCIAL STUDIES

Have students make a bartering bulletin board. Decide with students ten classroom privileges, such as watering the plants, delivering messages, and holding the door. Have volunteers draw a picture of each privilege, and label and post it on the board. Next give each student three strips of colored paper. Students write on the strips what services they will exchange for the classroom privileges they would like. Then students thumbtack their strips to the privileges they want. Decide if you will accept each student strip in exchange for the privilege. When the barter is complete, have students take their strips off the board.

Skill Work

TEACH/REVIEW VOCABULARY

To reinforce the meaning of vocabulary words, make up a simple crossword puzzle with clues for students to fill out. Invite students to make up their own simple crossword puzzles for other students to complete. Post the completed crossword puzzles on the bulletin board.

ELL To help students gain familiarity with vocabulary, have them write simple riddles for each vocabulary word. Encourage students to share their riddles with each other.

TARGET SKILL AND STRATEGY

SEQUENCE Remind students that *sequence* is the order in which events occur. Ask students to make diagrams of the sequence of events for getting ready for and going to school, starting with "I wake up" and ending with "I enter my classroom." Invite students to illustrate each stage of their diagrams.

SUMMARIZE Remind students that *summarizing* means briefly retelling the key points of a story or of a series of events. Ask students to summarize a story they have recently read or a movie or TV program they have recently seen.

ADDITIONAL SKILL INSTRUCTION

DRAW CONCLUSIONS Remind students that *drawing conclusions* means thinking about facts and details and deciding something about them. Before students read the book, ask them to skim the pages and look at the examples of bartering through time. Ask students if they can draw any conclusions about the benefits of bartering, given that the ancient system of bartering still goes on today.

Sequence

• The **sequence** of events in a story is the order in which the events occur.

1. What is the sequence of events that goes on in bartering?

_____

_____

_____

2. Describe the bartering that took place between the American colonists and Native Americans.

_____

_____

_____

3. Describe the sequence of events in "Bartering Day" at school.

_____

_____

_____

4. Trace the steps the community theater took to advertise its summer play.

_____

_____

_____

5. Look at the bartering plan on pages 8 and 9. Write down a sequence of events for how the Smith family might barter with the Jones family.

_____

_____

_____

_____

Vocabulary

Directions Unscramble each vocabulary word. Then write it on the line provided.

Check the Words You Know

___carpenter	___carpetmaker	___knowledge	___marketplace
___merchant	___plenty	___straying	___thread

1. acrpenter _____

2. gdnkowlee _____

3. ketplmarace _____

4. tylpen _____

5. ingtsray _____

6. readth _____

7. erpetcarmak _____

8. chantmer _____

Directions Complete each sentence with a word from the box.

9. The _____ is full of people buying and selling goods.

10. We have _____ of apples to bake a pie.

11. My mom used _____ to stitch the hole.

12. The skilled _____ tried to persuade me to buy one of his pictures.

Directions Write the definition of each vocabulary word below.

13. carpenter _____

_____

14. straying _____

_____

15. carpetmaker _____

_____

16. knowledge _____

_____

Ice Fishing in the Arctic

SUMMARY In this nonfiction selection, readers learn about Arctic ice fishing and the Inuit people of Nunavut, Canada. Students learn about the way of life in the Arctic Region of the world.

LESSON VOCABULARY

gear	parka
splendid	twitch
willow	yanked

INTRODUCE THE BOOK

INTRODUCE THE TITLE AND AUTHOR Discuss with students the title and author of *Ice Fishing in the Arctic*. Have students look at the cover art. Ask: What is this person doing? What do you think this nonfiction selection will be about?

BUILD BACKGROUND Discuss with students their experiences with fishing. Talk about how fishing in the Arctic might be different from fishing in other locations.

PREVIEW/USE TEXT FEATURES As students preview the book, encourage them to look closely at the pictures, photos, and maps. Ask students to note the information these pictures, photographs, and maps provide. Point out the clothing, fishing equipment, and environment.

READ THE BOOK

SET PURPOSE Have students set a purpose for reading *Ice Fishing in the Arctic*. Invite them to ask questions about the title, such as "What is Arctic ice fishing?" Students' curiosity about this topic should guide their purpose.

STRATEGY SUPPORT: VISUALIZE Explain to students that *visualizing* is forming pictures in their minds about what is happening in the story. Tell students that visualizing can help them understand and remember the text. Tell students that if they are not able to completely visualize an imagine to reread the passage or story to complete the picture.

COMPREHENSION QUESTIONS

PAGES 3 What are the grandfather and grandson going to do? *(They are gathering supplies that they will use to ice fish for their dinner.)*

PAGE 4 Where is the Arctic region? *(north of Canada)*

PAGE 7 How is ice fishing different from other kinds of fishing? *(You have to drill a hole in the ice, use a lure to attract the fish, and then catch it with a spear.)*

PAGE 12 For some Inuit people, what is another source of income connected to ice fishing? *(Many Inuit people are guides who take tourists out ice fishing.)*

REVISIT THE BOOK

READER RESPONSE

1. Possible responses: 1. Drill a hole in the ice. 2. Use a chisel to make the hole wider. 3. Attach the lure to a pole or branch, and then drop the lure through the ice into the water. 4. Twitch the lure to attract hungry fish. 5. Spear the fish through the ice hole.

2. Answers will vary but might include "Is it hard to catch fish by ice fishing?"

3. You twitch the lure to attract hungry fish.

4. Answers will vary but should include a reason why the student would like or dislike ice fishing in the Arctic.

EXTEND UNDERSTANDING Point out that sometimes authors use graphic sources like time lines, graphs, or maps to help the reader understand information in the text. Have students look again at the maps on pages 4 and 13. Discuss how the maps add to their understanding of the text.

RESPONSE OPTIONS

WRITING Have students imagine that they are touring the Arctic region and are going ice fishing with a guide. Ask them to write a journal entry about their first day and include at least three questions that they don't want to forget to ask their guide.

SCIENCE CONNECTION

Suggest that students find out more about Arctic animals and how they live in this region. Provide a selection of books and magazines about Arctic animals. Have students compare and contrast two Arctic animals.

Skill Work

TEACH/REVIEW VOCABULARY

Talk with students about how some of the words in the text create mood. Ask: How does the use of the word *parka* make you feel? How does the use of the word *splendid* to describe the winter day make you feel? Suggest that volunteers find the vocabulary words used in the selection and make up their own sentences using these words.

ELL Review vocabulary words with students. Personalize each word by asking them questions such as, "If you were in a parka, would you be hot or cold?" Do the same for the remaining vocabulary words.

TARGET SKILL AND STRATEGY

SEQUENCE Review with students that sequence is the order in which events happen in a story or selection. Remind students that sometimes an author uses clue words such as *first, second, then, next, finally,* and *last* to show sequence, but sometimes the author may not. Have students look for sequence clue words as they read.

VISUALIZE Remind students that it is important to form pictures in their minds to help them understand the story. Tell students to reread a passage when they cannot completely visualize their picture. Model using page 7. Say: I am picturing an Inuit in a large fur jacket, drilling a hole in the ice. I cannot picture what the Inuit will do next. After rereading the passage, I can also visualize the Inuit dropping a fishing lure into the dark hole.

ADDITIONAL SKILL INSTRUCTION

AUTHOR'S PURPOSE Remind students that authors always have a purpose, or reason, for writing. Point out that authors often write with more than one purpose. Based on the genre *(nonfiction)* and title of this book, *Ice Fishing in the Arctic,* ask: What do you think was the author's main purpose for writing? *(to inform the reader about Arctic ice fishing)* Challenge students to find at least one other purpose the author may have had for writing the selection.

Name _____

Sequence

- **Sequence** is the order in which things happen in a story or selection—what happens first, next, and last.

Directions Read the following passage. Answer each question below.

Darla wanted to go on an ice fishing trip. Darla decided she also wanted to buy a new parka. She needed to save some money, and fast!

Darla decided to make a savings plan. First, she set a goal. She figured out how much money she wanted to save. She thought that $100 would cover everything.

She knew that the trip was in two months. Darla earned about twenty dollars a week from her allowance and babysitting. She planned to save fifteen dollars a week. That would give her enough money for the trip. Finally, Darla went to the bank. She opened a savings account there. Her money would earn interest while it was in the bank.

1–3. How did Darla make her savings plan? Use sequence clue words to show the steps.

_____

_____

_____

_____

_____

4–6. What is the sequence of events in the passage? Use clue words to show the order.

_____

_____

_____

_____

_____

_____

Vocabulary

Directions Fill in the crossword puzzle using the clues and vocabulary words below.

Check the Words You Know
___gear ___twitch ___parka ___willow ___splendid ___yanked

Across

1. a kind of tree with long, flexible branches

5. to have pulled or jerked suddenly

6. equipment

Down

2. excellent or highly enjoyable

3. to move with a slight jerk, either once or repeatedly

4. a thick, fur-lined, hooded coat

Directions Select two vocabulary words and write a sentence for each one.

8. _____

_____

9. _____

_____

The Shopping Trip

SUMMARY In this fictional story, a young girl and her father go shopping for their family and end up with a new pet.

LESSON VOCABULARY

laundry	section	shelves
spoiled	store	thousands
traded	variety	

INTRODUCE THE BOOK

INTRODUCE THE TITLE AND AUTHOR Discuss with students the title and author of *The Shopping Trip*. Have students look at the cover art. Ask: What are the girl and her father doing? What do you think this story will be about?

BUILD BACKGROUND Discuss with students their experiences grocery shopping with an adult. Ask students if they have ever created a shopping list. Talk about how shopping with a list might be different from shopping without a list.

PREVIEW/TAKE A PICTURE WALK As students preview the book, encourage them to look closely at the illustrations and ask what information about the story these illustrations provide. Point out the expressions on the characters' faces, and ask students how this helps them understand what might be going on in the story.

READ THE BOOK

SET PURPOSE Have students set a purpose for reading *The Shopping Trip*. Students' interest in shopping may guide this purpose. Suggest that students think about how they shop for groceries.

STRATEGY SUPPORT: BACKGROUND KNOWLEDGE

Tell each student to create a KWL chart with the headings, What I Know, What I Would like to Know, and What I Learned. As a class, fill in the first column of the chart with what students already know about shopping and grocery stores. Then have individual students fill in the second column of the chart with topics they would like to know about shopping and grocery stores. Tell students that when they have finished reading, they will complete the third column with what they learned from the selection.

ELL Ask students to note words they don't understand. Suggest that they work with a partner to look up the word in a dictionary, write the meaning in their notebooks, and reread the part of the story where the word was used to check their understanding.

COMPREHENSION QUESTIONS

PAGE 3 What do we find out about Casey's new baby sister, Rose? *(Rose has been home for one week, she doesn't want to sleep, and she is keeping everyone else from sleeping too.)*

PAGE 4 What did the family do on Saturdays before baby Rose was born? *(They used to sleep late, eat pancakes, relax, and do their favorite activities.)*

PAGES 9 AND 10 What steps did Casey and her dad take to complete the shopping list at the grocery store? *(First they went to the dairy section, next to the diaper aisle, then to the deli counter, and finally to the cash register.)*

PAGE 14 What happened in the story that was a mix-up? *(Dad thought that goldfish meant a pet goldfish, but Mom wanted goldfish-shaped crackers.)*

REVISIT THE BOOK

READER RESPONSE

1. Before Rose: sleep late, eat pancakes, relax, do favorite activities; After Rose: Mom and Dad are tired. Casey is daydreaming about life before Rose. There isn't any food in the refrigerator.

2. Response will vary but should include prior knowledge that is applied to the story.

3. imperfect by damage or decay

4. Dad bought the goldfish by mistake because he did not understand or clarify what the word *goldfish* meant on the shopping list.

EXTEND UNDERSTANDING Remind students that *setting* is the time and the place of a story. Suggest that students go through the story and write down details in the text and art that show where and when the story takes place. Ask: Where does the story take place? When does the story take place?

RESPONSE OPTIONS

WRITING Have students create a shopping list and then write a paragraph describing their shopping adventure. Ask them to detail the steps they would take to complete their shopping trip.

SOCIAL STUDIES CONNECTION

Time For SOCIAL STUDIES

Collect weekly grocery sales flyers from the newspaper and, using the food pyramid, have students create a healthy meal plan for a week that includes grains, vegetables, fruits, dairy products, meats, and beans.

Skill Work

TEACH/REVIEW VOCABULARY

Invite students to make a word web for each vocabulary word. Have them supply at least two words that they associate with each vocabulary word.

TARGET SKILL AND STRATEGY

COMPARE AND CONTRAST Explain to students that to *compare* and *contrast* is to look for likeliness and differences between objects, ideas, or pieces of text. Call attention to how the family has changed on page 4. Model comparing and contrasting by asking questions such as "What is different about Casey's family since Rose was born? What is the same?"

BACKGROUND KNOWLEDGE Tell students that thinking about what they already know about a topic can help them understand what they read. Suggest that if students use *background knowledge,* they will be able to make better generalizations about the facts in the text. As students read, have them note at least one instance where they activate background knowledge to help them understand the text.

ADDITIONAL SKILL INSTRUCTION

CHARACTER Remind students that characters are people or animals in stories. Tell them that sometimes authors do not tell everything about their characters. Students can also learn about characters from characters' words and actions. Explain that students can use these clues to predict what a character will do next. Have students read the text on page 4. Ask: What do Casey's thoughts tell you about Casey? *(Students should see that Casey thinks that Rose has changed everything.)* Then have students read the first paragraph of page 13. Ask: What do Casey's thoughts and actions tell you about Casey? *(Casey kisses Rose because she loves her little sister.)*

Compare and Contrast

- When you **compare** two or more things, you think about how they are alike and how they are different.
- When you **contrast** two or more things, you only think about how they are different.

Directions Look back at the selection *The Shopping Trip*. Compare and contrast the family before and after Rose was born.

Before Rose was born	After Rose was born
1. _____	3. _____
_____	_____
_____	_____
2. _____	4. _____
_____	_____
_____	_____

5. What remained the same before and after the Rose was born?

_____

_____

_____

_____

Vocabulary

Directions Write the word from the box that best completes each sentence.

Check the Words You Know
___laundry   ___traded   ___store   ___shelves
___spoiled   ___section   ___variety   ___thousands

1. You would not want to eat food if it is _____.

2. We had four loads of _____ to wash, dry and put away.

3. We needed milk, bread and cheese from the _____.

4. Long ago, people bartered for goods and often _____ things.

5. There was a _____ of fruits and vegetables on the table.

6. We found yogurt, milk and cheese in the dairy _____ of the grocery _____.

7. Cereal, soup, and diapers were on the grocer's _____.

8. We looked in and were amazed to see _____ of shoppers at the store for the sale.

Directions Write two sentences, using as many vocabulary words as you can. Make sure the sentences make sense.

9–10. _____

_____

_____

_____

_____

_____

_____

The Market Adventure

SUMMARY This is a fictional story about a family who has moved to Mexico from the United States. It gives students information about different settings and shows how characters might act in a new setting.

LESSON VOCABULARY

arranged	bundles
dangerously	errands
excitedly	steady
unwrapped	wobbled

INTRODUCE THE BOOK

INTRODUCE THE TITLE AND AUTHOR Discuss with students the title and the author of the book *The Market Adventure*. Direct students' attention to the cover illustration and ask them what the illustration makes them imagine the story might be about.

BUILD BACKGROUND Discuss if students have ever lived in a different culture, have visited a new place, or have tried new foods. Ask: How did that make you feel? Discuss with students if they have ever read any books about different countries and what they might have learned.

ELL Ask students to share their experiences of coming to a new culture. Discuss American food items that were new to them.

PREVIEW/USE ILLUSTRATIONS Invite students to look at the illustrations throughout the book and ask what information about the story these illustrations give them. Point out the expressions on the characters' faces, and ask students how this helps them understand what might be going on in the story.

READ THE BOOK

SET PURPOSE Have students set a purpose for reading *The Market Adventure*. Their curiosity about living in a strange land and buying exotic vegetables should help guide this purpose.

STRATEGY SUPPORT: STORY STRUCTURE Suggest that students make a story map, labeled *Beginning, Middle,* and *End,* and have them fill in story details for each section. Discuss with students how the story would be changed if any of the events were put into a different order.

COMPREHENSION QUESTIONS

PAGE 3 What is the first problem of the story, and what is the plan to solve it? *(Dad needs a chili pepper, and Amelia goes out into the new neighborhood to get one.)*

PAGES 6–7 Use the illustrations to describe the setting of the open-air market. *(The streets are colorful, and there are vendors everywhere.)*

PAGE 14 What words would you use to describe Amelia? *(Possible responses: curious; adventuresome; excited)*

REVISIT THE BOOK

READER RESPONSE

1. The author's purpose is to inform and entertain.
2. Pots and pans wobbled on a stand; a man bought a sombrero; Amelia bought a chili pepper.
3. Possible responses: standing/stand, chopping/chop, living/live, seeing/see, walking/walk, selling/sell, going/go, doing/do, talking/talk, shopping/shop
Sentences will vary.
4. Possible response: I would like to go to the Carribean to study the Taino culture. I like Taino music.

EXTEND UNDERSTANDING Remind students that *dialogue,* or speech, is what characters say to each other. Suggest that students look at the dialogue on page 15 when Amelia says, "Our shopping has been a great success." Discuss why Amelia says that and what it shows about her character.

RESPONSE OPTIONS

WRITING Suggest that students imagine they are Amelia and are writing letters home to the United States about their first weeks in Mexico. Have volunteers read their letters to the class.

SOCIAL STUDIES CONNECTION

Time For
SOCIAL
STUDIES

Suggest that students research another country and its food. Then invite students to write a short story about going to a market to buy that food.

Skill Work

VOCABULARY

Review vocabulary words with students. Provide sentences in which the vocabulary words have been used incorrectly, and ask students to correct the sentences.

TARGET SKILL AND STRATEGY

AUTHOR'S PURPOSE Tell students that an author may write for different purposes—to inform, to persuade, to entertain, or to express feelings. Based on their previews, ask students what they think the *author's purpose* was for writing *The Market Adventure.*

STORY STRUCTURE Remind students that stories are arranged in a sequence with a beginning, a middle, and an end. Discuss how stories usually have a problem that must be solved before the end. Suggest that as students read, they map out the *story structure*, writing down what the problem is, how it is being solved, and what happens at the end of the story. Remind students that understanding the story structure can also help them understand the characters and the setting.

ADDITIONAL SKILL INSTRUCTION

GENERALIZE Remind students that a *generalization* is a broad statement that applies to many examples. Clue words like *everyone, always, in general,* and *none* can help students identify generalizations. Remind students that not all generalizations are true, especially if there are no facts to support them; for example: All classical music is played loudly. Then suggest that students make generalizations about what they read.

Author's Purpose

- The **author's purpose** is the reason or reasons an author has for writing.
- An author may have one or more reasons for writing. He or she may want *to inform, to persuade, to entertain,* or *to express* a mood or feeling.

Directions Read the passages and write the purpose you think the author had for writing each.

1. Casey's baby sister Rose had been home for just one week. But already, Casey's excitement was wearing off.

_____

2. Casey zipped right over to the puppies. Her heart melted. Oh, *if only*—but, Casey knew that now was not a good time to plead for a puppy.

_____

3. "Where are the crackers?" Mom said. A silly grin spread across Dad's face. He held up a clear plastic bag half-filled with water. In it swam a bright orange goldfish.

_____

4. **Directions** Write a short paragraph about family. Choose one purpose for your paragraph. Write so that your purpose will be easily understood.

_____

_____

_____

_____

_____

Vocabulary

Directions Find the misspelled vocabulary word or words in each sentence and correct them. Then write a sentence of your own using the same vocabulary words.

<table>
<tr><th colspan="4">Check the Words You Know</th></tr>
<tr><td>___arranged</td><td>___bundles</td><td>___dangerously</td><td>___errands</td></tr>
<tr><td>___excitedly</td><td>___steady</td><td>___unwrapped</td><td>___wobbled</td></tr>
</table>

1. Amelia completed all of her erands at the market and unrapped her packages

   when she got home. _____ _____

   _____

   _____

2. "I love chili peppers!" said Ben excitly. _____

   _____

   _____

3. The salesperson sorted the fruit neatly into big bundels. _____

   _____

   _____

4. The pile of pots and pans was not stedy and wobbled dangresly.

   _____ _____

   _____

   _____

Directions Write a short paragraph about a character you make up. Use as many vocabulary words as you can.

_____

_____

_____

_____

These Birds Can't Fly!

SUMMARY Birds that cannot fly can still thrive in different environments. This book introduces the reader to flightless birds from around the world. It explains how key characteristics help the emu, flightless cormorant, and others meet their survival needs.

LESSON VOCABULARY

cuddle	flippers
frozen	hatch
pecks	preen
snuggle	

INTRODUCE THE BOOK

INTRODUCE THE TITLE AND AUTHOR Discuss with students the title and the author of *These Birds Can't Fly!* Ask: What can you learn about flightless birds by looking at the cover photograph? Talk about what information students think the author will provide based on the title and cover.

BUILD BACKGROUND Have students think about birds with which they are familiar. Ask students where they have seen birds—including outdoors, TV, and the zoo. Discuss what students have noticed about birds. Ask students if they think there are skills other than flying that can help birds move and survive.

PREVIEW/USE TEXT FEATURES Point out that the photographs on pages 3, 5, and 14 are paired for specific reasons. Ask students how pairing the photos helps illustrate important ideas on each page.

READ THE BOOK

SET PURPOSE Have students set a purpose for reading *These Birds Can't Fly!* This purpose should be guided by the impressions they get from skimming the photos, captions, and maps, along with their own curiosity.

STRATEGY SUPPORT: MONITOR AND CLARIFY Remind students that rereading and reviewing can help them answer their questions about text, find the main idea, and restore comprehension when their understanding breaks down. Tell students that seeking help from teachers and peers can further boost their problem-solving skills. Encourage them to help each other and learn how to ask good questions by providing opportunities for cooperative work.

COMPREHENSION QUESTIONS

PAGE 3 Contrast flightless birds with flying birds. *(Flightless birds have heavier bones and their feathers are different from those of flying birds.)*

PAGES 5–6 How are ostriches and emus alike and different? *(Both ostriches and emus eat plants. Ostriches live in Africa, and emus live in Australia.)*

PAGES 6, 11 How do birds such as emus and flightless cormorants meet their needs without the ability to fly? *(Emus have powerful legs, and flightless cormorants can swim well. This allows them to move quickly and survive.)*

PAGES 8–9 What does the map tell you about flightless birds? *(Different varieties live all over the world.)*

REVISIT THE BOOK

READER RESPONSE

1. Possible responses: Main Idea: there are many kinds of flightless birds; Detail: penguins; Detail: ostriches; Detail: emus
2. Responses will vary but might include monitoring and clarifying by rereading, reviewing text, and finding the main idea of a paragraph or passage.
3. Possible responses: He climbed through the ship's *hatch* to get on deck. He decided to *hatch* a plan to get the money.
4. the flightless cormorant of the Galápagos Islands

EXTEND UNDERSTANDING Have students look at the map on pages 8–9. Discuss how the call-outs draw attention to specific species of flightless birds and where they live. Then ask how the call-outs would change if the map focused entirely on flying birds and their habitats. What would the call-outs show and where would they point? Students may use reference sources to gather information on flying birds.

RESPONSE OPTIONS

WRITING Ask: If you could be any flightless bird, which one would you be and why? Have students answer in one or two paragraphs.

ELL Invite students to draw a picture of a flightless bird and write labels or captions for its body parts.

WORD WORK Challenge students to write or verbalize sentences that incorporate two or more vocabulary words. Provide an example, such as, *The penguin chicks snuggle and cuddle with their mothers to stay warm.*

SCIENCE CONNECTION

Invite students to use reference sources to learn more about what characteristics help flightless birds thrive.

Skill Work

TEACH/REVIEW VOCABULARY

Have volunteers demonstrate their knowledge of vocabulary words by acting them out and/or incorporating them into sentences.

TARGET SKILL AND STRATEGY

MAIN IDEA AND DETAILS Tell students that the *main idea* is the most important idea about the topic. To find it, students must determine the relative importance of information they read. *Supporting details* are pieces of information that tell more about the main idea. Model how to ask questions to find the main idea of a book. Ask: In a word or two, what is this book about? (This identifies the topic.) What is the most important idea about the topic? (This identifies the main idea.) What are some details that tell more about the main idea? As students read, have them think about the main idea.

MONITOR AND CLARIFY Remind students to use clarifying strategies such as rereading and reviewing to restore their understanding when problems arise. Encourage students to use this strategy when their understanding of the text breaks down. They may also reread if they have a question after reading. Remind students to use teacher-directed questioning in small groups to reinforce the importance of rereading to find information. Tell them that using this strategy to monitor comprehension on their own will help them find the main idea of the selection.

ADDITIONAL SKILL INSTRUCTION

COMPARE AND CONTRAST Tell students that to *compare* is to identify how two or more things are alike, whereas to *contrast* is to identify how they are different. Ask students to compare and contrast aspects of flightless birds in the book, such as their natural habitats. Suggest that students use a chart to keep track of similarities and differences.

Main Idea and Details

- The **main idea** is the most important idea about a paragraph, passage, or story.
- **Details** are pieces of information that tell more about the main idea.

Directions Read the following passage. Then answer the questions below.

> Birds that cannot fly are called flightless birds. They differ from flying birds in many ways. The bones of flightless birds are heavier than those of flying birds. Flightless birds' feathers are also different from those of flying birds. Like humans, all birds have a breastbone. However, a flightless bird's breastbone is different from that of a flying bird since it has no flight muscles attached.

1. In one or two words, what is this paragraph about?

_____

2. What is the main idea of the paragraph?

_____

_____

3. What is one important detail that tells more about the main idea?

_____

_____

4. What is another important detail about the main idea?

_____

_____

5. What is a third detail about the main idea?

_____

_____

Name _____

Vocabulary

Directions Read each numbered vocabulary word and the four words that follow it. Circle the two words that are synonyms for the vocabulary word.

Check the Words You Know
__cuddle   __flippers   __frozen   __hatch
__pecks   __preen   __snuggle

1. cuddle

slaps   hugs   throws   snuggles

2. flippers

eyes   paddles   fins   noses

3. frozen

chilly   icy   melted   burned

4. hatch

fall   fly   produce   cause

5. pecks

strikes   walks   swims   hits

6. preen

see   dress   groom   laugh

7. snuggle

nestles   avoids   holds   kicks

Directions Write a paragraph about penguins using at least four vocabulary words.

_____

_____

_____

_____

Iguana Takes a Ride

SUMMARY Iguana needs to cross the river to get to his mother. The boatman offers to take him, but Iguana thinks his price is too high. Crocodile swims up and offers to take Iguana for free across the river. Iguana asks other animals what he should do; all edge away from Crocodile. When a frog accepts Crocodile's offer, Iguana sees him become a single bite for Crocodile. Iguana decides to take the boatman's ride and tells him, "I'd rather be safe than sorry."

LESSON VOCABULARY

adorable	compassionate
exactly	iguana
mature	mention
trophies	

INTRODUCE THE BOOK

INTRODUCE THE TITLE AND AUTHOR Discuss with students the title and the author of *Iguana Takes a Ride*. Based on the title and cover art, ask students to describe what they think this book will be about.

BUILD BACKGROUND Ask students if they have ever had to make a decision about getting home. Discuss with them when such a decision might be necessary, perhaps when they've stayed too long at a friend's or relative's house. Tell them that Iguana uses good judgment to make an important decision.

PREVIEW/USE ILLUSTRATIONS Have students skim through the book, looking at the pictures. Ask: What do you think the story is about? Who are the characters? Where does the story appear to take place?

READ THE BOOK

SET PURPOSE Have students set a purpose for reading *Iguana Takes a Ride*. This purpose should be guided by the impressions they get from reading the title and skimming the illustrations along with their own curiosity.

STRATEGY SUPPORT: VISUALIZE Remind students that we can *visualize*, or get a picture in the mind's eye, when we read. Explain that the other senses—hearing, taste, smell, and touch—as well as sight can help to create these pictures, which make what we read seem more real. Tell them that they will be able to form pictures if they use prior knowledge about crocodiles and other animals of the jungle as they read.

COMPREHENSION QUESTIONS

PAGE 4 What kinds of skills does the boatman tell Iguana he possesses? *(He promises a safe ride, says he handles a boat well, and that his boat can ride rough waves.)*

PAGE 6 What does the boatman tell Iguana when Crocodile offers to take Iguana across the river for free? *(He tells Iguana to be careful because crocodiles are not known to be compassionate.)*

PAGE 8 Which is the only animal to tell Iguana that Crocodile can be trusted? *(Crocodile's mother)*

PAGE 11 Why does the frog talk to the boatman before he hops onto Crocodile's back? *(Possible response: He too thinks that the boatman charges too much and that he will accept Crocodile's offer to carry him for free.)*

REVISIT THE BOOK

READER RESPONSE

1. Boatman: safe ride, skilled boater, five dollars; Crocodile: uncertain ride, free; Both: will carry Iguana across the river and know how to make their way in the water
2. Responses will vary based on what students have read and experienced.
3. *Compassionate* is found on page 6 and means that someone cares about or is sympathetic to someone else.
4. Responses will vary but should reflect the importance of using good judgment when there is a possibility of risk involved in making a decision.

EXTEND UNDERSTANDING Discuss with students that *plot* refers to the events in a story that carry the story from beginning to middle to end. Point out that Crocodile and his mother act friendly toward Iguana but that the other animals try to avoid Crocodile, so Iguana takes his time making a decision. Discuss with students that the frog who accepted Crocodile's offer moved the story toward the end.

RESPONSE OPTIONS

WORD WORK Challenge students to write or verbalize sentences that incorporate two or more vocabulary words. Provide an example, such as this: *Though Crocodile's mother said that her son was adorable, Iguana believed that something wasn't exactly right about his offer.*

SCIENCE CONNECTION

Provide appropriate nonfiction books about crocodiles and their prey, and invite students to use reference sources to learn more about how crocodiles survive and thrive along waterways. Have them share what they learn with the class.

Skill Work

TEACH/REVIEW VOCABULARY

Read the vocabulary words. Ask students about words they may already know. Discuss how they first heard of the words and what they think the words mean. Tell them that they will become more familiar with these words as they read.

TARGET SKILL AND STRATEGY

COMPARE AND CONTRAST Tell students that when we *compare* two or more things, we look to see how they are alike and perhaps how they are different. When we *contrast* two or more things, we are concerned only with how the things are different. Ask students to name the characters they can compare and contrast (the boatman and the Crocodile, Iguana and the frog, Iguana and the other animals). Have students create Venn diagrams to compare and contrast the characters they choose to examine.

VISUALIZE Tell students that when they *visualize,* they form a picture in their minds about what they are reading. This picture may be helped along by illustrations in what they are reading, the words the author uses to describe things, and prior knowledge about the topic of the text they are reading.

ELL Reread page 15 with students and talk about the main idea of the story. (It's better to be safe than sorry. Also, some students may say, "You get what you pay for.")

ADDITIONAL SKILL INSTRUCTION

DRAW CONCLUSIONS When students *draw conclusions,* they should use what they read and what they already know to figure out more than what is presented in the book. Use graphic organizers to model how to draw conclusions—a chart with columns for facts from the book, what I already know, and the conclusions that result. Have students share facts and prior knowledge while drawing conclusions about what they read in the book.

Compare and Contrast

- To **compare** is to see how two or more things are alike and different.
- To **contrast** is to see how two or more things are different.

Directions In *Iguana Takes a Ride,* you learned about how Iguana made his decision to cross the river. In the chart below, compare and contrast the boatman with Crocodile. Be sure to list the things Iguana considered about each character.

Boatman	Crocodile
1. _____	3. _____
2. _____	4. _____

5. What made Iguana decide to go with the boatman? Write a paragraph to explain.

_____

_____

_____

_____

Vocabulary

Directions Below each vocabulary word is a row of four words or phrases. Circle two that have almost the same meaning as the vocabulary word.

Check the Words You Know

___adorable	___compassionate	___exactly	___iguana
___mature	___mention	__trophies	

1. adorable

lovable   ugly   cute   harsh

2. compassionate

mean   sympathetic   selfish   understanding

3. exactly

just so   off the mark   approximately   precisely

4. iguana

tropical plant   tropical lizard   tropical bird   animal with tail

5. mature

composed   full-grown   childlike   tiny

6. mention

keep quiet   speak about   say quickly   shout

7. trophies

jackets   prizes   desks   awards

The Last Minute

SUMMARY A girl named Katy puts off reading a book for an assigned book report. When she is forced to finish her book and write about it during one very stressful weekend, Katy vows to never again leave any assignment until the last minute.

LESSON VOCABULARY

butterflies	collection
enormous	scattered
shoelaces	strain

INTRODUCE THE BOOK

INTRODUCE THE TITLE AND AUTHOR Discuss with students the title and the author of *The Last Minute*. How does the cover illustration support the title? What situations might the author have in mind for Katy based on these elements?

BUILD BACKGROUND Have students discuss situations in which they put off assignments or tasks until the last minute. What challenges did they face while trying to meet their deadlines?

PREVIEW/USE TEXT FEATURES As students look through the illustrations, have them focus on the characters' poses and facial expressions. Then discuss what they think the characters are doing.

READ THE BOOK

SET PURPOSE Have students set a purpose for reading *The Last Minute*. This purpose may be guided by students' own experiences with completing school assignments at the last minute. Ask them to think about what they learned from these experiences and what Katy, the main character of the book, might learn from hers.

STRATEGY SUPPORT: QUESTIONING Remind students that asking good questions about important text information in a story is a good way to become a better reader. *Questioning* can take place before, during, and after reading a story. After previewing and setting a purpose for reading *The Last Minute*, encourage students to ask themselves a question to keep in mind as they begin. Model: I wonder what this will be about.

COMPREHENSION QUESTIONS

PAGE 4 Katy's friend, Pam, began working on her book report early. How do you think Pam's report turned out? Why? *(Possible response: Pam's report probably turned out well because she gave herself enough time to finish it.)*

PAGES 6–10 What drew Katy's attention away from writing her report? In what order did these activities happen? *(Katy was first distracted by soccer practice, then by watching TV, and then by working on a coin collection, the need to clean up her room, and a soccer game.)*

PAGE 15 What did Katy promise to do after she handed in her book report? Why? *(Katy promised to never leave anything until the last minute again because cramming for her book report was so stressful.)*

REVIST THE BOOK

READER RESPONSE

1. Possible evidence: Pam read her book right away; she suggests that Katy go to the library to get a book; tells Katy that she always leaves things until the last minute. Possible conclusion: Pam plans ahead and is also a very good friend.

2. Answers will vary but should reflect the confusion and regrets that Katy's procrastination caused her.

3. The base words are *inform* and *collect*. Possible sentences: When are you going to inform your teacher of your book selection? Chris decided to collect baseball cards.

4. Possible answer: Start my homework earlier.

EXTEND UNDERSTANDING Tell students that a *plot* is an organized pattern of events in a story. Use simple story maps with students to help them determine and note the most important events of the story. For example, point out that Katy's soccer game on page 10 is important because it is yet another obstacle that prevents Katy from writing her report on time, whereas the place where her teammates decide to have ice cream afterward is not important to the pattern of the story.

RESPONSE OPTIONS

WRITING Tell students that Katy might have had fewer problems if she had created and followed a timetable of things to do for her book report. Invite students to select a real-life assignment with a deadline and create a timetable of things they must do in order to meet the deadline.

WORD WORK Create sentences with each of the vocabulary words, but leave a blank space where each vocabulary word should be. Provide students with a word bank of vocabulary to complete the sentences.

SOCIAL STUDIES CONNECTION

Many people face deadlines as part of their daily routines. Discuss what kinds of jobs involve deadlines and why it is important for people with those jobs to manage their time carefully.

Skill Work

TEACH/REVIEW VOCABULARY

Ask students to find how each vocabulary word is used in the book. Encourage them to use the illustrations for clues to define the vocabulary in their own words.

TARGET SKILL AND STRATEGY

DRAW CONCLUSIONS Explain to students that an author may not tell exactly what a story is about but leave it up to the reader to figure out, or *draw a conclusion. The Last Minute,* for instance, almost gets lost in details about Katy and her book report. Ask students to tell what they believe is the most important idea behind this story.

QUESTIONING Have students revisit and answer the questions they asked themselves before they began to read *The Last Minute.* Then have them generate a final question, such as *I wonder what the author wanted me to remember from this story.*

ELL Ask students to identify words in the book that they are struggling with. Help them create a glossary based on these words.

ADDITIONAL SKILL INSTRUCTION

SEQUENCE Tell students that a story's *sequence* tells the order in which events occur. Using sequence skills to keep track of which events happened first, next, and last is essential for a correct understanding of books such as *The Last Minute.* Ask volunteers to explain how the events of the beginning and middle of the story have a dramatic effect on its ending.

Draw Conclusions

- When you **draw a conclusion,** you think about facts and details and decide something about them.

Directions Read the following passage from *The Last Minute.* Insert one fact about Katy in the first box and another fact about her in the second box. Write your conclusion in the last box.

Tuesday came, and Katy watched TV for a few hours after school. Then she worked on her coin collection until bedtime. She loved her shiny coins.

"It's too late to read now," she decided. "Tomorrow I'll start it for sure."

Pam told her she couldn't come over after school the next day. "I have to work on my book report. Are you liking your horse book?"

"I'm going to start it today," Katy said.

"Boy!" Pam exclaimed. "You always leave things until the last minute!"

"It's not the last minute," Katy told her. "I still have four whole days left."

That night Katy had to clean her room. When she finished, she was too tired to read. The next night she could only understand a few pages before she went to sleep.

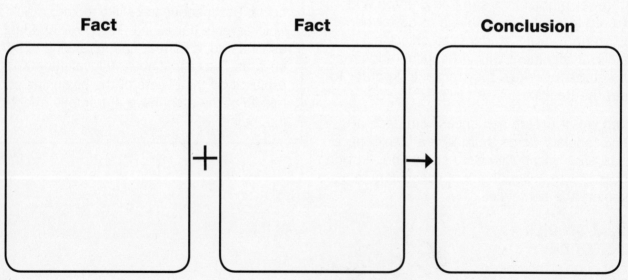

Fact   **Fact**   **Conclusion**

Vocabulary

Directions Read each numbered vocabulary word and the four words that follow it.
Circle the two words that are synonyms for the vocabulary word.

Check the Words You Know

| ___butterflies | ___collection | ___enormous |
| ___scattered | ___shoelaces | ___strain |

1. butterflies

wings insects flutters Monarchs

2. collection

group set scattering book

3. enormous

huge tiny medium giant

4. scattered

grouped separated sprinkled sorted

5. shoelaces

ribbons soles ties shoestrings

6. strain

achieve try strive complete

Directions Write a paragraph that includes at least four of the vocabulary words.

_____

_____

_____

_____

_____

_____

Our Garden

SUMMARY This is a story about how a group of schoolchildren transforms an empty urban lot into a beautiful garden. They get the entire community involved, which brings both beauty and a fresh community spirit to the town.

LESSON VOCABULARY

bottom	cheat
clever	crops
lazy	partners
wealth	

INTRODUCE THE BOOK

INTRODUCE THE TITLE AND AUTHOR Discuss with students the title and the author of *Our Garden*. Based on the title, ask students to describe any images they may have about the story. Suggest students also look at the cover illustration. Ask: How does this picture relate to the title?

BUILD BACKGROUND Discuss with students what they know about planting. Ask them if they understand what is involved in growing plants. Discuss any projects students have done in groups, such as decorating the classroom for a holiday or preparing a group report, and whether it was easier to complete the project when everyone worked together.

ELL Invite students to share words from their home languages related to planting or gardens. Post these words on a bulletin board beside the English words.

PREVIEW/USE ILLUSTRATIONS As students preview the book, suggest that they notice how the artwork shows groups of people, rather than individuals. Discuss why students think the artist did this. Ask them to note the title of the story, *Our Garden,* and to discuss how it connects to the illustrations.

READ THE BOOK

SET PURPOSE Have students set a purpose for reading *Our Garden*. Students' interest in gardening or plants should guide this purpose. Suggest that students also consider how working together for a common good can help their own community.

STRATEGY SUPPORT: PREDICT As students read about the group working to transform the lot into a community garden, tell them that predicting can give them a chance to use what they already know to make connections with what will happen next. Predicting also allows them to make sense of the story and gives them a stake in the outcome. Encourage students to write their predictions and to check them against what happens in the story.

COMPREHENSION QUESTIONS

PAGE 4 Why would a garden give the old lot new life? *(Possible response: A garden is full of growing, living things.)*

PAGE 5 Why do you think Mayor Smith is so excited about the garden? *(Possible response: He knows the children's garden will benefit the whole community.)*

PAGE 9 How do the workers at City Hall help with the garden? *(They collect money and pay for the plants, seeds, and soil needed for the garden.)*

PAGE 15 What is the author's purpose in writing a story about a whole community getting involved in a project? *(Possible response: She wants to show how everyone has fun and benefits from working together.)*

REVISIT THE BOOK

READER RESPONSE

1. Possible response: to show how rundown the lot had become and how much work the kids needed to do
2. Possible response: People will see what a lovely spot the lot has become and will help take care of the garden.
3. Possible response: *crops* as a verb means "to shorten." Possible sentence: The haircutter *crops* five inches off the child's hair.
4. Possible response: don't litter, no loud music, no fighting, no dogs allowed in the garden

EXTEND UNDERSTANDING Remind students that the *setting* is the time and the place where a story takes place, and that the setting can affect what happens in the story and why. Discuss with students whether this particular story could have happened in any other time or place. If so, would it have had the same end results? Discuss with students how the story would be different if it had happened in a very small country village, for example, or in the year 2233.

RESPONSE OPTIONS

WORD WORK Discuss with students their reaction to the word *community*. In this story, the community is a town and its people. Ask students if they know any other kinds of communities or organizations. Make a diagram with students about the class community. The diagram should show who is in the community and how they work together for the common good of the whole classroom.

SCIENCE CONNECTION

TIME FOR Science

Students can learn more about how plants grow by growing their own bean plants from seeds in the classroom. Suggest that students make a chart with assigned jobs for watering, tracking growth, cleaning up loose soil, and other gardening tasks. Post the chart in the classroom.

Skill Work

TEACH/REVIEW VOCABULARY

To reinforce the contextual meaning of the vocabulary words, ask students to write sentences using each word. Then invite students to build a *word wall* where they will come up with other words that have to do with plants. Suggest that students position these words on the wall so that they form a picture that resembles a growing plant with many leaves and branches.

TARGET SKILL AND STRATEGY

AUTHOR'S PURPOSE Remind students that every author writes a story for a *purpose,* or reason, such as to entertain, give information, persuade, or teach. Ask students why they think the author wrote this story. Suggest that as students read, they track and make note of any story details that might support their answers.

PREDICT Remind students that to *predict* means to guess what you think might happen next in a story based on what has already happened. Suggest that students pause once or twice while they read the story to make predictions about what is going to happen. Then they can see whether their predictions were right, as they continue to read.

ADDITIONAL SKILL INSTRUCTION

PLOT Remind students that *plot* is the series of events in a story. Instruct students that as they read, they should look for a problem or conflict that the story is posing. Then they can figure out what is happening in the beginning of the story, the middle of the story, and at the end of the story, when the conflict is resolved.

Author's Purpose

- The **author's purpose** is the reason or reasons the author has for writing.
- To *inform, persuade, entertain,* or *express* are common reasons for writing.

Directions Answer the questions.

1. Why do you think the author gave so many details about how everyone cleaned up the empty lot?

_____

_____

_____

2. Why do you think the author wrote a book about a group of people building a garden rather than just one person?

_____

_____

_____

3. Explain why one of the purposes the author may have had was to inform.

_____

_____

_____

4. How did the author show she also wanted to entertain?

_____

_____

_____

5. In what way did the author try to persuade?

_____

_____

_____

Name _____

Vocabulary

Directions Find the vocabulary word that matches each clue below.

Check the Words You Know			
___bottom	___lazy	___cheat	___partners
___clever	___wealth	___crops	

1. It means a large amount of something, usually money. _____

2. It means the opposite of hardworking. _____

3. It means the opposite of top. _____

4. If someone is dishonest, he or she might do this. _____

5. We use this word to describe a person who likes to lie around all day. _____

6. We use this word to describe kinds of plants you grow to eat. _____

7. This word is used to describe someone who is smart. _____

8. If you and somebody else are these, you work together toward a goal. _____

Directions Write a sentence that uses two of the vocabulary words.

_____

_____

_____

_____

Bills and Beaks

SUMMARY This book gives readers information about birds and the importance of their beaks and bills. Students will learn how birds feed, protect, and care for themselves using their beaks and bills.

LESSON VOCABULARY

bill	goo
hunters	material
platform	tons
twigs	

INTRODUCE THE BOOK

INTRODUCE THE TITLE AND AUTHOR Discuss with students the title and author of *Bills and Beaks*. Have students look at the cover photograph. Ask: What kind of animal is this? What do you think you might read about in this book?

BUILD BACKGROUND Engage students in a discussion about what they know about birds. Ask: How do birds use their bills and beaks? Ask them if they have ever had a bird as a pet, observed a bird in the zoo, or watched one in nature.

ELL Ask students who have visited or lived in other countries to describe birds they may have seen there and compare them to local birds.

PREVIEW/TAKE A PICTURE WALK Have the students preview the book, looking at the pictures. Look specifically at the photographs on pages 4 and 5 and ask the students to describe what they see. Also encourage them to explore the other photographs and make predictions about the text.

READ THE BOOK

SET PURPOSE Based on your discussion of the cover and the picture walk, invite students to share what about this book makes them interested in it. Ask: What do you know about birds and their beaks? What do you want to learn about birds and their beaks?

STRATEGY SUPPORT: TEXT STUCTURE Remind students that text structure is the way an author organizes information to help readers understand the text. *Bills and Beaks* is structured using descriptions. Each section describes the birds with a particular kind of beak. The book informs and uses photos and captions to make information easy to read. Explain to students that they should think about and use the text structure of *Bills and Beaks* as they read.

COMPREHENSION QUESTIONS

PAGE 4 Birds' beaks are made of keratin. What other two things mentioned in the text are made of keratin? *(fingernails and horses' hooves)*

PAGE 6 What do birds do with their bills? *(Birds use their bills to eat, talk, and sing. Birds use their bills to pick up and carry nesting material, to build their nests, to clean themselves.)*

PAGE 9 How does a woodpecker use its bill? *(Possible response: A woodpecker uses its bill as a drill to make a hole in a tree.)*

PAGE 11 The text says that eagles, hawks, and owls are hunters. Look at the pictures in the book. What other birds are hunters? *(The heron stabs frogs and the robin eats worms.)*

REVISIT THE BOOK

READER RESPONSE

1. The main idea is that birds can do incredible things with their bills, or beaks. Details: Responses will vary but should be taken from the book.
2. Responses will vary.
3. *branch, stick*
4. Responses will vary.

RESPONSE OPTIONS

WRITING Invite students to write a few sentences describing their favorite bird, paying particular attention to the bird's beak or bill. Provide art materials and have students illustrate their sentences.

SCIENCE CONNECTION

Create a bulletin board showing the different kinds of birds and their beaks and bills. Have students draw or find photographs that represent each category of beak and bill. Place students in four groups and ask each group to write a few sentences about one type of beak. Work together to display the pictures and sentences on a bulletin board.

Skill Work

TEACH/REVIEW VOCABULARY

Create a set of cards with the vocabulary words printed on them. Create another set of cards with these synonyms of the vocabulary words: *beak, glop, seekers, stuff, raised area, plenty, branches.* Show each synonym card and read it aloud. Students can practice matching the correct word with its synonym, saying the words as they do.

TARGET SKILL AND STRATEGY

MAIN IDEA AND DETAILS Remind students that the *main idea* is the most important idea about a paragraph, passage, or article. Details that support the main idea tell the reader more about that idea. Ask: What is this book about? (This identifies the topic.) What is the most important idea about this topic? (This identifies the main idea.) Ask students to list or tell some of the details they have read that back up the main idea.

TEXT STRUCTURE Remind students that text structure is the way a text is organized. Recognizing internal structure can help students focus on the text and better understand what they read. Explain that in this book, the author structures each selection using descriptions. Have students take notes about the descriptions as they read.

ADDITIONAL SKILL INSTRUCTION

SETTING Point out to students that the setting is where and when a story takes place. Since this is not a story but is instead a factual account, it has no true setting. Instead, it discusses the natural habitat of each bird by questioning the details in the photos and the information provided in the text. For example, the hummingbird needs to live in a warm climate where flowers grow.

Main Idea and Details

- The **main idea** is the most important idea about a paragraph, passage, or story.
- **Details** are small pieces of information that tell more about the main idea.

Directions Read the following passage. Then answer the questions below.

Birds have bills in all sorts of shapes and sizes. Birds do all sorts of things with their bills, from picking up nest materials to using the bills as tools. They use their bills to keep themselves clean, which helps them fly.

But the most important thing a bird uses its bill for is to feed itself. In fact, the size and shape of a bird's bill can tell you a lot about what it eats. Birds' bills have adapted, or changed, over millions of years.

1. Use two or three words to tell what this passage is about.

_____

2. What is the main idea of the passage?

_____

3. What is one detail that tells more about the main idea?

_____

_____

4. What is another detail that tells about the main idea?

_____

_____

5. What is a third detail about the main idea?

_____

_____

Vocabulary

Directions Write the word that best completes each sentence. Some words will be used more than once.

> ## Check the Words You Know
>
> ___bill   ___goo   ___hunters   ___material
> ___platform   ___tons   ___twigs

1. A hummingbird has a long, narrow _____.

2. A swan scoops up fish and _____ in its bill.

3. The mother bird used _____ to build her nest.

4. The eagle flew up to its nest on a _____.

5. The _____ of the nest was twigs, leaves, string, and grasses.

6. The birds that caught frogs in their beaks were _____.

7. A bird eats, breathes, and sings with its _____.

8. There were _____ of insects for the birds to eat.

9. The _____ was a mix of seaweed, small fish, and pond water.

10. The _____ in the nest were neatly braided into a home.

Directions Write two to three sentences about birds using as many vocabulary words as possible.

_____

_____

_____

_____

_____

In the Fields

SUMMARY Students read about a fictional family of migrant farm workers picking grapes in California in 1965. Family members become involved in the grape-pickers' strike in 1965 that ultimately led to better working conditions.

LESSON VOCABULARY

area	artificial
grapevines	preservative
proof	raise
raisins	

INTRODUCE THE BOOK

INTRODUCE THE TITLE AND AUTHOR Discuss the title and author of *In the Fields*. Based on the title and the illustration on the cover, ask students to predict what they think this book might be about.

BUILD BACKGROUND Discuss with students why some people sometimes hold up signs for others to see. Help them realize that often the sign carriers want others to know they object to some actions of other people.

PREVIEW/USE TEXT FEATURES After students have previewed the book, discuss what they think the story is about based on the illustrations. Point out that the illustration on page 3 shows people picking grapes in a field. Ask: What is different about page 16?

READ THE BOOK

SET PURPOSE Have students set a purpose for reading *In the Fields*. Ask them to consider what it might be like to pick grapes with their family.

STRATEGY SUPPORT: IMPORTANT IDEAS Explain to students that good readers recognize which ideas they read are the most important ones. Point out that not every idea they read is important. Tell them that as they read they should try to figure out which are the most important ideas. Model questions to ask while reading, such as: Is this idea important enough to remember? Or is this idea just a small detail?

COMPREHENSION QUESTIONS

PAGE 3 Why do you think the water in the fields is not safe for Luis and his father to drink? *(It is probably dirty water that people have been walking through.)*

PAGE 4 What must it have been like for families like Luis's to work in the grape fields and live in those shacks without running water or refrigerators? *(Answers will vary, but students will likely conclude that the living conditions must have been terribly uncomfortable.)*

PAGES 8–12 What did Tonio want Luis's father to do? *(join him and others to go on strike)* What did they hope to have happen when they went on strike? *(They hoped that the owners of the fields would need them to work so badly that they would agree to give the workers better working conditions.)*

REVISIT THE BOOK

READER RESPONSE

1. Possible response: The family has a difficult life, since they all work in the fields and live in a shack.
2. Responses may vary, but students should list important ideas.
3. A context clue within the same sentence as the word *preservative* on page 5 explains that it would keep the raisins fresh so they would keep for a long time. Students' sentences will vary.
4. Possible response: Luis's mother was afraid they would lose their jobs and the money they earned.

EXTEND UNDERSTANDING Explain to students that workers going on strike is something people still feel strongly about. Sometimes it does result in companies agreeing with what the strikers want because the companies need the people to work. Sometimes companies hire other people to work, and the strikers don't get what they want.

RESPONSE OPTIONS

SPEAKING Divide students into two teams. Have one team decide among themselves what might be good about workers like Luis's family going on strike, and the other team to think about reasons why it's not a good idea. Have the teams present their positions to the whole class.

DRAMA CONNECTION

Using the story of Luis and his family as an example, have students work together to put on a short play about workers in the grape fields and their situation in the 1960s. Point out that students can include information from page 16 in their play. Have volunteers take parts, decide on the plot and action, and present the play for another class.

Skill Work

TEACH/REVIEW VOCABULARY

Tell students that homophones are pairs of words that sound alike but do not have the same spelling or meaning. Write *raise* on the board, use it in a sentence, and ask students to think of a homophone for it. Ask a volunteer to use *rays* in a sentence. Then ask students to use the other vocabulary in a sentence.

ELL Provide students with other examples of homophones such as *allowed/aloud, ant/aunt, bee/be, choose/chews,* and *main/ mane*. Discuss the meanings of each word and help students use each one in a sentence. Invite them to add any examples of homophones in their home language.

TARGET SKILL AND STRATEGY

DRAW CONCLUSIONS Remind students that they can add what they already know to information they read to *draw conclusions*. Model by saying: I read that Luis had to work all day without clean water. After spending a day in the sun I am very thirsty. Not providing water for Luis made his working conditions difficult.

IMPORTANT IDEAS Review with students how to choose the most important ideas from text. Reread page 4, ask: What is the main idea of this page? What details support this idea?

ADDITIONAL SKILL INSTRUCTION

AUTHOR'S PURPOSE Explain to students that every person who writes a book has a reason for writing it. Discuss possible reasons Michele Spirn wrote *In the Fields*. Ask: What do you think she wanted you readers to know and to think about? What makes you think so?

Draw Conclusions

- **Drawing conclusions** means adding what you already know to something you read to make a decision about something.

Directions Read the following passage. Then answer the questions that follow.

Many workers who moved around picking grapes and other crops were like Luis's family. They were paid very little money. They had to live in very poor conditions provided by the owners of the fields where they worked. Most of these workers spoke very little English. They had trouble finding other kinds of work in this country.

1. What were two of the uncomfortable and unfair conditions the workers had?

_____

_____

_____

2. How would you and your family feel if you had to live with these conditions?

_____

_____

_____

3. What can you conclude about why the workers agreed to go on strike with César Chávez in 1965?

_____

_____

_____

Name _____

Vocabulary

Directions Find the misspelled word in each sentence and write it correctly. Then write a sentence of your own that includes that word.

Check the Words You Know

___area   ___artificial   ___grapevines   ___preservative
___proof   ___raise   ___raisins

1. Don't water those artifical flowers!   _____

    _____

2. The aera we live in gets a lot of rain.   _____

    _____

3. A preservitive helps raisins last a long time.   _____

    _____

4. Grapvines grow around the top of the gate.   _____

    _____

5. Rasins are a good snack.   _____

    _____

6. The championship game will riase a good crowd.   _____

    _____

7. A fact that proves something is true is prof.   _____

    _____

The Thunder and Lightning Men

SUMMARY This fictional text tells a Passamaquoddy legend of how thunder and lightning occur and their origin.

LESSON VOCABULARY

antlers	narrator
imagined	overhead
languages	poked

INTRODUCE THE BOOK

INTRODUCE THE TITLE AND AUTHOR Discuss the title and author of *The Thunder and Lightning Men.* Based on the title and the illustration on the cover, ask students to predict what they think this book might be about. Ask: What makes you think this book is fiction?

BUILD BACKGROUND Point out to students that thousands of years before we actually knew what caused such things as thunder and lightning, most groups of people made up stories called legends that told what people believed explained them.

PREVIEW/USE TEXT FEATURES After students have previewed the book, discuss what they think the story is about based on the illustrations. Ask: How do the pictures help you predict the events in the story?

READ THE BOOK

SET PURPOSE Have students set a purpose for reading *The Thunder and Lightning Men.* Discuss whether they think they will learn any facts in the story and why.

STRATEGY SUPPORT: INFERRING Tell students that good readers often "read between the lines" to figure out a lesson in the text. Explain that they can combine what they read with what they already know to create an idea of their own.

COMPREHENSION QUESTIONS

PAGE 4 When the chief thought a place needed thunder and lightning, what did he do? *(He called the thunder and lightning men together and told them where to go and how long to be gone.)*

PAGES 5–6 What did the man have to do to become a thunder and lightning man? *(He had to go through a ceremony during which he entered a big box where he lost all his senses. When he came out, he received his wings and bow and arrow.)*

PAGES 11–15 What happened when the man began to miss his family? *(He remembered the things he did with his family. He finally told the chief that he wanted to go home. The chief had the thunder and lightning men take him home.)*

REVISIT THE BOOK

READER RESPONSE

1. Possible response: Characters: chief, man The chief gave the man wings and a bow and arrow so he could become a thunder and lightning man.
2. Possible response: The man seemed to enjoy being a thunder and lightning man. Understanding that helps explain why he stayed there so long.
3. Sentences will vary, students should correctly use the vocabulary words.
4. Responses may vary, but should relate to the story.

EXTEND UNDERSTANDING Tell students that legends are not as important to modern people, now that scientific fact has shown us what actually causes such things as thunder and lightning. Now we read legends to entertain and to help us understand how people thought long ago.

RESPONSE OPTIONS

WRITING Invite students to make up their own legend that explains something in nature, such as night and day or winter and summer. Have them write several paragraphs to tell their story. Ask volunteers to share their legends with the class.

ELL Ask volunteers from other countries to write or tell a legend from their own culture that explains something in nature.

SOCIAL STUDIES CONNECTION

Provide a map that shows the state of Maine and the province of New Brunswick in Canada. Show students the area where the Passamaquoddy lived. Then display a map that shows the area where you live. Ask students to discuss what they know about the Native Americans who lived where they do.

Skill Work

TEACH/REVIEW VOCABULARY

Explain to students that context clues can help them define words they do not understand. Use page 3 as an example. Ask: What clue in the sentence explains what a narrator is? *(a person who tells a story)* Write the other vocabulary words on the board and work with students to develop a sentence for each word that contains a context clue to its meaning.

TARGET SKILL AND STRATEGY

CHARACTERS, SETTING, AND PLOT Recall with students that characters are the people in a story, the *setting* is when and where the story takes place, and the *plot* tells what happens. Discuss the characters, setting, and plot of *The Thunder and Lightning Men* by asking: Where did this story take place? Who was in the story? What happened in the story?

INFERRING Discuss with students that *inferring* is using what they already know to learn something new. Model this by saying: I knew that Native Americans told legends. I read how the Passamaquoddy people believed thunder and lightning were created. I learned that legends helped the Native Americans explain how natural occurrences happened. Ask students to share other inferences they made while reading.

ADDITIONAL SKILL INSTRUCTION

COMPARE AND CONTRAST Recall with students that *comparing* means showing how things are alike and that *contrasting* means showing how they are different. Suggest that students compare and contrast this story's explanation of thunder and lightning to one in their science textbook or an encyclopedia.

Characters, Setting, and Plot

- **Characters** are the people in a story.
- **Setting** is where and when a story happens.
- **Plot** is what happens in a story: the beginning, the middle, and the end.

Directions Think about the story *The Thunder and Lightning Men.* Answer the questions about its characters, setting, and plot that follow.

1. Who were the two main characters in the story?

_____

_____

2. Where did the story take place?

_____

_____

3. When did the story take place?

_____

_____

4. In the boxes below, describe the beginning, middle, and end of the story.

Beginning	**Middle**	**End**

Name _____

Vocabulary

Directions Write the vocabulary word that completes each sentence. Underline the context clue or clues to the meaning of the word.

> ## Check the Words You Know
> ___antlers   ___imagined   ___languages
> ___narrator   ___overhead   ___poked

1. The huge _____ on the deer's head seemed very heavy.

2. Reach up high to put your suitcase in the _____ compartment of the airplane.

3. The baby laughed when I _____ my finger into his tummy.

4. The play we saw included a _____ who explained what was happening.

5. The new girl in school is from Holland, and she speaks four _____ besides English.

6. I saw the pictures in my head as I _____ what it would be like to be a thunder and lightning man.

Directions Choose two of the vocabulary words. Write your own sentence for each one. Try to include a context clue to the word's meaning.

7. _____

_____

8. _____

_____

Meet the Stars

SUMMARY This story is about a young boy, Arnie, who has just moved from the city to a small town and is invited to view the stars and constellations at his new neighbor's home. The story also shows students how people can learn to adapt to new surroundings and environments.

LESSON VOCABULARY

dim	gas
gigantic	ladle
pattern	shine
temperature	

INTRODUCE THE BOOK

INTRODUCE THE TITLE AND AUTHOR Discuss with students the title and author of *Meet the Stars*. Have students look at the cover. Ask: Why do you think this book is called *Meet the Stars*? What clues about the story's content do you see in the cover illustration?

BUILD BACKGROUND Engage students in a discussion about what they know about astronomy. Ask students if they have ever looked at the stars through a telescope or gone to a planetarium. Also ask students what they know about stars, planets, or the sun and moon.

PREVIEW/TAKE A PICTURE WALK Have students preview the book, looking at the pictures. Look specifically at the illustration on page 13 and ask students to describe what they see. Also encourage them to explore the other illustrations and make predictions about the text.

READ THE BOOK

SET PURPOSE Based on your discussion of the cover and the picture walk, invite students to share what about this book makes them interested in it. Ask: What do you know about star-watching? What do you want to learn about stars and constellations?

STRATEGY SUPPORT: STORY STRUCTURE While students read about how Arnie is learning to like his new town, they should follow the story structure to help them keep track of its overall meaning. Explain that following a story from beginning to end will help students distinguish between plot and detail.

COMPREHENSION QUESTIONS

PAGE 3 What does Arnie conclude about his new house? What information is he basing his conclusion on? *(Arnie concludes that his new house is the worst place ever because of the dark clouds, spooky house next door, and rain.)*

PAGE 9 How does Arnie feel about the invitation? *(Arnie is excited about the invitation from a boy his own age but thinks that the stars are Hollywood stars.)*

PAGE 14 What star is closest to Earth? *(the sun)*

PAGE 15 How does Arnie's attitude change at the end of the story? *(Arnie is no longer bored and likes his new home.)*

REVISIT THE BOOK

THINK AND SHARE

1. Responses will vary but should include why the illustrations did and did not help.
2. Responses will vary but should include how Arnie's feelings changed.
3. Three synonyms are *enormous, massive,* and *immense.*
4. Responses will vary but should show understanding of the story.

RESPONSE OPTIONS

WRITING Have students learn about a constellation or planet and write a paragraph about it. Then have them illustrate their paragraphs. Display students' work in the classroom.

SCIENCE CONNECTION

Create a bulletin board of an evening sky map showing several different constellations. Have students draw or find photographs that represent each constellation. Ask students to label each star pattern.

Skill Work

TEACH/REVIEW VOCABULARY

Review the vocabulary words. Then play Vocabulary Master with students. Give students three definitions for each vocabulary word, including one that is "far out" or silly. Then have them select the correct definition. Students can use each word in a sentence.

ELL Review vocabulary words with students. Then have them make a simple puzzle of the vocabulary words that uses the definitions as clues.

TARGET SKILL AND STRATEGY

GRAPHIC SOURCES Tell students that as they read *Meet the Stars,* to create two or three graphic organizers to enhance their understanding of the story. For example, they could use a story map for the plot; a time line for the sequence of events; character webs to describe Arnie, Ms. Williston, or Thomas; or a problem-and-solution or cause-and-effect chart to understand the action in the story.

STORY STRUCTURE Explain to students that the *story structure* is how the story is organized, and that a story has a beginning, middle, and an end. Discuss with students how this story might look similar to other stories. Tell students to think about what the beginning, middle, and end might be as they read.

ADDITIONAL SKILL INSTRUCTION

PLOT Remind students that a *plot* is the sequence of events that takes a story from the beginning to the middle to the end. A plot is often about how someone solves a problem. Ask students to map the plot of a story they have recently read, dividing the events into *beginning, middle,* and *end.* Suggest that the students trace the plot of *Meet the Stars* as they read the story.

Graphic Sources

- **Graphic sources** present information visually and can help you better understand the text.
- Graphic sources include chart, diagrams, maps, and pictures with captions.

Directions Study the timeline. Then fill in the sequence of events below.

Meet the Stars

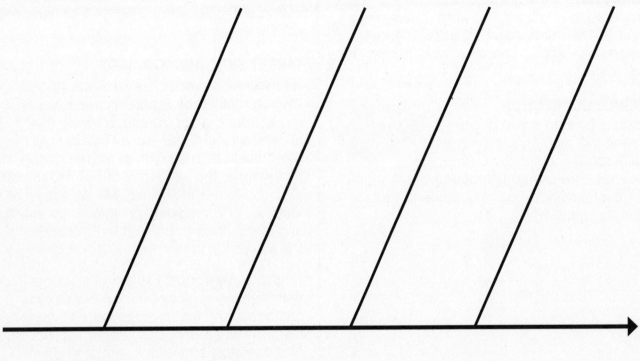

| **1.** First | **2.** Next | **3.** Then | **4.** Last |

1. First, _____

_____

2. Next, _____

_____

3. Then, _____

_____

4. Last, _____

_____

Vocabulary

Directions Fill in the crossword puzzle using the clues and the words in the box.

Check the Words You Know

| ___dim | ___gas | ___gigantic | ___ladle |
| ___pattern | ___shine | ___temperature | |

Across

3. lacking brightness

4. an order or arrangement

6. a serving scoop for liquids

7. combustible substances or fuels

Down

1. huge

2. glowing

5. the degree of heat

Directions Write a sentence using two or more vocabulary words.

_____

_____

What a Day!

SUMMARY Dana likes to help her mom, a veterinarian at an animal shelter. On this snowy day, Dana spends her time with the dogs. Her favorite part is showing the dogs to people who want to adopt them. Dana also finds a lost dog in the snow—just in time.

LESSON VOCABULARY

anxiously	bay	blizzards
channel	chipped	melody
supplies	surrounded	symphony

INTRODUCE THE BOOK

INTRODUCE THE TITLE AND AUTHOR Discuss with students the title and the author of *What a Day!* Based on the title, discuss with students how this book might be related to the concept of helping animals in danger. Ask if students can tell by the title and cover illustration if it is a fiction or nonfiction book.

BUILD BACKGROUND Discuss what students know about animal shelters, and ask if any of them have adopted animals from one. Encourage students to describe their experiences at shelters and how people helped the animals there.

PREVIEW/USE ILLUSTRATIONS Suggest that students look at the illustrations to predict how the story will tell about a day with dogs. By looking at the pictures, can they describe how the girl helps the dogs?

READ THE BOOK

SET PURPOSE If necessary, go back to the material presented in Build Background to generate ideas from students as to why they may want to read this book. Most children like animals and may be interested in reading about other children helping them. Suggest that students may want to make up their own animal story after reading this one.

STRATEGY SUPPORT: STORY STRUCTURE Tell students that *story structure* is the way a story is organized and that this story tells the events in the order in which they happened, or in sequence. Ask students to make a story map, labeled *Beginning, Middle,* and *End,* and have them fill in the story details for each section. Discuss with students how the story would be changed if any of the events were put into a different order.

COMPREHENSION QUESTIONS

PAGE 7 Why does Maria say that the dogs were wailing? *(They don't like the weather.)*

PAGE 9 What was difficult for Dana when she helped at the shelter? *(when dogs she loved were adopted)*

PAGE 13 Why did Dr. Tran wrap the lost dog in a blanket? *(The dog needed warmth.)*

PAGE 14 Even though the dog did not have a collar, why didn't Dana think he was a stray? *(Dana was careful to observe how the puppy looked and acted, and that made her wonder if the owner missed the dog.)*

REVISIT THE BOOK

READER RESPONSE

1. Possible responses: a pace for people to bring strays; a place for the strays to be sure they don't harm people; a place where people can adopt a pet for free; a place where people who love animals can volunteer.
2. Possible response: First, Dana volunteered at the animal shelter. Then, Dana helped with the dogs and supplies. Finally, Dana rescued and returned Inky to his owners.
3. Possible response: Dana was worried about the dog getting back to its owners.
4. Possible response: The chip identified the dog's owners; without it, the dog would have had to stay at the shelter.

EXTEND UNDERSTANDING Students may want to think about themselves as if they were in the character's place. Help students see that authors often write characters so that the reader can identify with them or want to be like them. Ask students what made the character of Dana believable. Their responses may help them in their writing the *Response Option*.

RESPONSE OPTIONS

WRITING Suggest that students use the questions they had from reading and research some aspect of caring for dogs or other animals in rescue situations. Divide the class into two groups—one group to write a story about children helping animals and another group to illustrate it.

SOCIAL STUDIES CONNECTION

Students may want to research shelters or seeing eye dogs. If possible, have stories available of dogs helping humans.

TEACH/REVIEW VOCABULARY

Talk with students about how some words in a story create mood. Ask: How does the use of *blizzard* bring urgency to the story? Why might the sounds of a *symphony* help dogs in a shelter? Suggest that volunteers find the vocabulary words used in the story and make up their own sentences using these words.

ELL Ask students to work in pairs, each writing a different word and its definition on either side of an index card. Less-proficient English speakers can gain more facility with the vocabulary words by saying the word and its definition with help from more-proficient speakers.

TARGET SKILL AND STRATEGY

GENERALIZE As students read the book, have them look for the specific ways Dana, her mother, and Dr. Tran help the dogs. Suggest that students track this information by putting it in a cluster diagram around a central idea of *humans helping animals*. Then ask students to *generalize* about how people help animals.

STORY STRUCTURE Share with students that stories are arranged in a sequence. Discuss how stories usually have a problem that needs to be solved. Suggest that as students read, they fill in their story map and write down what the problem is, how is it solved, and what happens at the end of the story. Explain to students that understanding the story structure can also help them understand the characters and setting.

ADDITIONAL SKILL INSTRUCTION

CHARACTER Help students begin to make inferences about Dana's *character* by listing their ideas of what kind of person she is.

Generalize

- When authors present one statement about many ideas or people, they are making a **generalization**.
- A generalization is a kind of conclusion.

Directions Use the graphic organizer to make a generalization based on *What a Day!* Choose three details from the list below that go together. Write them in the Supporting Details boxes. Then write a generalization in the top box.

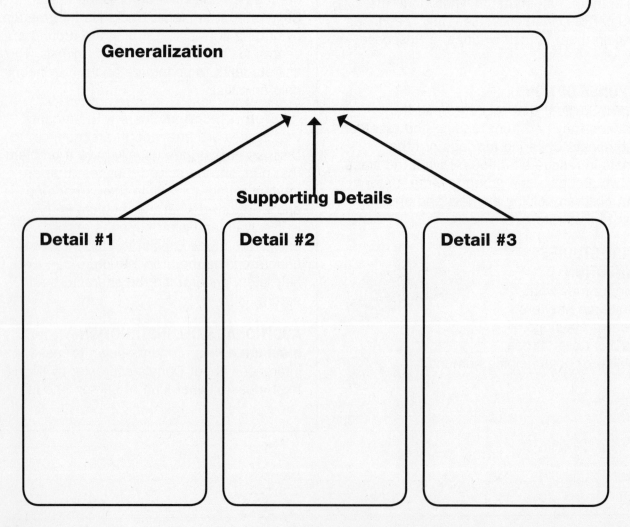

Story Details
- Dana introduces people to dogs waiting to be adopted.
- Dana is put in charge of dogs.
- The dogs cry in bad weather.
- Dana helps Maria all morning.
- identification chip
- Many dogs race to greet Dana.
- blizzard coming
- Dana spends time with each dog.
- Dana saves a puppy in the snow.
- Shy Elvis sits on Dana's lap.
- Dogs become quiet when Dana comes.

Generalization

Supporting Details

Detail #1

Detail #2

Detail #3

Vocabulary

Directions Read the sentences. Write the word from the box that means the same as the underlined word or phrase.

Check the Words You Know

___ anxiously	___ bay	___ blizzards
___ channel	___ chipped	___ melody
___ supplies	___ surrounded	___ symphony

1. _____ Dana wanted to play a <u>simple tune</u> on a flute.

2. _____ Dana did not see any boats in the <u>narrow water passage</u>.

3. _____ All the dogs <u>encircled</u> Dana, begging for her attention.

4. _____ Dana's mother <u>scraped</u> the ice off her car windows.

5. _____ "This is scary," said Dana as she looked at the <u>snowstorm</u> outside.

6. _____ Dana felt sad to see that the dogs waited <u>nervously</u> in their cages for food and water.

7. _____ The whistling wind seemed to create a <u>whole concert</u> of sounds from nature.

8. _____ Marie made sure the veterinarians had the <u>necessary goods</u> to care for the sick animals.

9. _____ Dana's house was set off the <u>inlet</u> and down the road from the river.

Directions Write one sentence about *What a Day!* using as many vocabulary words as possible.

10. _____

_____

Desert Life

SUMMARY This nonfiction selection describes some of the plants and animals that live in deserts.

LESSON VOCABULARY

incredible	lofty
noble	search
sting	survivors
topic	unseen
waterless	

INTRODUCE THE BOOK

INTRODUCE THE TITLE AND AUTHOR Discuss the title and author of *Desert Life*. Have students look at the cover photograph and tell what kind of animal and plant they see.

BUILD BACKGROUND Invite students to tell what they know about deserts, including what a desert is. If you live in a desert area of the Southwest, have students describe features they have observed.

PREVIEW/USE TEXT FEATURES Have students preview the book by paging through it and looking at the photographs. Ask: What makes you think this book is nonfiction? What does the map and chart on page 14 tell you about deserts? How can the captions and glossary help you?

READ THE BOOK

SET PURPOSE Suggest that students think of something they want to know about animals and plants that live in a desert. That will help them set a purpose for reading *Desert Life*.

STRATEGY SUPPORT: PREDICT AND SET PURPOSE Remind students that they can be better readers if they predict what a book will be about and choose a purpose for reading it. Point out that they can use such text features as illustrations and captions to help them predict what a book will be about. After they have made their predictions, they can consider what their purpose will be. For example, predicting that *Desert Life* includes information about desert plants and animals could help students set the purpose of learning facts about them.

COMPREHENSION QUESTIONS

PAGE 3 How is the Mojave Desert different from other areas of the United States? *(It is very dry and hot. Plants and animals there must adapt to the harsh conditions.)*

PAGES 4–5 How are the two kinds of cactus described on these pages alike? How are they different? *(They both grow very tall and they store water to use between rainfalls. The pancake prickly pear has pads that look like pancakes where it stores water. The saguaro holds water in its expanded ribs and long root. It can live 200 years.)*

PAGES 6–13 What do some desert animals do to help themselves survive in the desert? *(Responses will vary but should reflect what students have read, such as hunting at night when it's cool, staying underground out of the sun, having bodies that store water, and so on.)*

REVISIT THE BOOK

READER RESPONSE

1. Possible response: Saguaro cactus: Cause: Not much water. Effect: Ribs expand to store water. Armadillo lizard: Cause: Reptiles, birds, or mammals hunt it. Effect: Rolls itself up.
2. If it never rained in the desert, all animals and plants would eventually die. Clues in the book list ways desert animals and plants conserve water.
3. Vocabulary words that can be used as adjectives include *incredible, lofty, noble, unseen,* and *waterless.* Sentences will vary.
4. Responses will vary. Make sure students can defend their choices with information they have read.

ELL These students may have difficulty with question 3. Explain that one test they can use to identify an adjective is to think about a noun that could come right after it. For example, they could think of an *incredible day, a lofty thought, a noble person, an unseen object,* or *a waterless desert.* If a noun can't come after the word and make sense, then it is not an adjective.

EXTEND UNDERSTANDING Point out to students that animals and plants in climates other than the desert also have adapted to their surroundings. As an example, you might want to mention the plants and animals that live on the floor of dense forests without much sun.

RESPONSE OPTIONS

SPEAKING Ask small groups of students to find out more about one of the plants or animals mentioned in the book. Have groups report their additional information to the whole class.

SCIENCE CONNECTION

Provide students with examples of several familiar plants and animals that are native to the climate you live in. Ask each student to write several sentences about one animal or one plant and the way it has adapted to its surroundings. If you live in a desert area, have students find an animal or plant that is not mentioned in the book to write about.

Skill Work

TEACH/REVIEW VOCABULARY

Brainstorm with students to use each vocabulary word in an oral sentence. Ask volunteers to remove the prefix from *unseen* and the suffixes from *lofty* and *waterless* and use the base words in oral sentences.

TARGET SKILL AND STRATEGY

CAUSE AND EFFECT Remind students that a *cause* is why something happens and an *effect* is what happens as a result of that cause. Model a cause-and-effect relationship by saying: The desert does not get much rain *(cause)* so the Saguaro cactus stores water *(effect).* Ask students to give several examples of cause and effect.

PREDICT AND SET PURPOSE Review with students what they predicted the book would be about and the purpose they set for reading it. Ask whether their predictions matched the content and whether they revised their purpose for reading as they went along. Remind them that changing their predictions and purposes as they need to is something good readers do.

ADDITIONAL SKILL INSTRUCTION

GENERALIZE Remind students that a *generalization* is an idea that describes many things that are alike in some way. Ask: What generalization could you make about the desert plants and animals you read about? *(They all adapted to living in the desert without much water.)*

Cause and Effect

- An **effect** is something that happens.
- A **cause** is what makes something happen.
- Sometimes there are clue words and phrases that can help you figure out what happened and why. Some examples are the words and phrases *because, so, since,* and *as a result.*

Directions Read each sentence. Underline the effect and write the cause.

1. Plants and animals survive in the desert because they adapt.

_____

2. Desert kangaroo rats sleep during the hot desert days so they can go out to find food at night.

_____

3. Because there is little water in the desert, cactus plants store water.

_____

4. If the armadillo lizard becomes frightened, it rolls itself up.

_____

5. Since the Gila monster hunts at night, it can't be seen very well.

_____

6. As a result of their ability to store water, desert tortoises can go for years without drinking.

_____

7. When it gets too hot, cactus wrens look for food in shady areas.

_____

8. Rain causes dramatic changes in the desert.

_____

Vocabulary

Directions Write the word that best completes each sentence. Check each word as you use it.

Check the Words You Know

___incredible   ___lofty   ___noble
___search   ___sting   ___survivors
___topic   ___unseen   ___waterless

1. Some animals move around the desert _____ at night.

2. Something that's hard to believe is _____.

3. Most animals spend a lot of time in _____ for food.

4. A desert is not completely _____.

5. Many kinds of plants and animals are desert _____.

6. The title of the book *Desert Life* gives its _____.

7. Some spiders will _____ insects to get food.

8. The very tall saguaro cactus looks _____.

9. A bird can look down on the desert from its _____ perch on a saguaro.

Directions Write a paragraph about desert plants or animals and use as many vocabulary words as possible.

_____

_____

_____

_____

_____

_____

A Trip

SUMMARY In this fictional story, a girl who loves basketball and is inventing a special shot has the opportunity to visit the Naismith Memorial Basketball hall of Fame, a real place in Springfield, Massachusetts.

LESSON VOCABULARY

basketball	disease
freeze	guard
popular	sports
study	terrible

INTRODUCE THE BOOK

INTRODUCE THE TITLE AND AUTHOR Discuss the title and author of *A Trip*. Ask students what they think is going on in the cover illustration. What sport do they think the book is about? Why?

BUILD BACKGROUND Explain that many sports have buildings that are Halls of Fame, where people who were special in the history of the game are honored.

PREVIEW/USE TEXT FEATURES Ask students to preview the book by paging through it and looking at the illustrations. Lead them to forecast what the book might be about. Ask students to predict the end of the story using the illustrations.

ELL Make sure all students understand something about the game of basketball before they proceed to read the book. Those from other countries, for example, may be unfamiliar with the game.

READ THE BOOK

SET PURPOSE Make sure students consider what they saw when they previewed the book to help them set a purpose for reading. Point out that although the story may be enjoyable, they might also learn something about basketball.

STRATEGY SUPPORT: SUMMARIZE Recall with students that *summarizing* means telling only the main ideas or events in a story, not the details. Good readers often summarize what they are reading as they go along to check their understanding. Tell students that after they finish reading, they should take a few minutes to summarize what they have read in their own minds.

COMPREHENSION QUESTIONS

PAGE 3 Why do you think Asha is working on developing a special basketball shot? *(She loves basketball and she wants to be better at it.)* Why does she call it the *r-t-f-f-s-s?* *(That's an abbreviation for reverse triple fake fadeaway scoop shot, which is what she has named her special shot.)*

PAGE 5 Where was Asha going with her father and little sister? *(The Naismith Memorial Basketball Hall of Fame)* Why do you think they were going there? *(Asha is very interested in basketball, and perhaps her father is, too.)*

PAGE 9 Who are the two basketball players in the illustration and why are they there? *(Manute Bol was the tallest professional basketball player at almost eight feet tall. Muggsy Bogues was the shortest player in National Basketball Association (NBA) history.)*

PAGE 13 Why does the Hall of Fame include a statue of James Naismith? *(because he invented the game of basketball)*

PAGE 14 Why do you think Asha wanted to keep her special move a secret? *(She wanted it to be perfect before she showed other people.)* Why did she change her mind when she and her sister played in the Hall of Fame building? *(Her dad wanted to see the play.)*

REVISIT THE BOOK

READER RESPONSE

1. Responses will vary, but many students will be able to generalize that most basketball players are tall.

2. Charts and summaries will vary, but summaries should include the points that Asha wanted to be a better basketball player, she was able to visit the Basketball Hall of Fame, she saw examples of many famous basketball players there, and she showed her dad her special play while she was there.

3. Sentences will vary. Note that *disease* is on page 3, *popular* on page 7, and *guard* on page 3.

4. Responses will vary, but make sure students explain why they like the sport so much.

EXTEND UNDERSTANDING Students may have heard of basketball great Michael Jordan and wonder why he isn't mentioned in the story. Explain that Jordan was inducted into the Hall of Fame in September of 2009, after this story was written. The NBA said, "By acclamation, Michael Jordan is the greatest basketball player of all time."

RESPONSE OPTIONS

WRITING Provide materials about the game of basketball and some of its famous players. Add Michael Jordan to those listed in the story. Have students choose a player to write about. Invite them to do some research, perhaps including the Internet. Then have them write a brief essay about the player and why he or she is so special.

SPORTS CONNECTION

Naismith invented basketball so students would have a game to play inside a gym during cold winter months. Work with students to name other indoor sports and games. Have volunteers explain how they are played. If possible, have students choose one to play in your school gym or on the playground.

Skill Work

TEACH/REVIEW VOCABULARY

Post the list of vocabulary words. Brainstorm with students to use each one in an oral sentence. Encourage students to include a context clue to the word's meaning if they can.

TARGET SKILL AND STRATEGY

GENERALIZE Remind students that when they make a broad statement that covers many different examples, they are generalizing. Point out that they may come across generalizations in their reading. Sometimes generalizations are identified with clue words such as *all, most, never, usually, generally,* and so on. Explain to students that generalizations should supported by observable facts or statements.

SUMMARIZE Remind students that when they summarize, they give just the main points of something they have read. List several details from a story students have read and ask them to explain why those would not be included in a summary of the story.

ADDITIONAL SKILL INSTRUCTION

GRAPHIC SOURCES Discuss with students that graphics such as illustrations, maps, charts, and so on can help them understand what is in a story or article. Have them discuss how the illustrations helped them understand what the Basketball Hall of Fame looks like. Ask: How did the map on page 16 help you figure out where the Hall of Fame is?

Generalize

- A **generalization** is a broad statement that applies to many examples.
  - Sometimes a generalization is signaled by a clue word such as *all, most, many, never, usually,* or *generally.*
  - A generalization should be supported by facts and be reasonable.

Directions Use the title of each section below to guide you. Write two facts about the title that you learned from the story *A Trip*. Then use those facts to make a generalization about basketball.

James Naismith

1. _____

2. _____

Naismith Memorial Basketball Hall of Fame

3. _____

4. _____

Wilt Chamberlain

5. _____

6. _____

Nancy Lieberman

7. _____

8. _____

Generalization about basketball

_____

_____

_____

_____

Name _____

Vocabulary

Directions Use each vocabulary word in a sentence as directed.

Check the Words You Know		
___basketball	___disease	___freeze
___guard	___popular	___sports
___study	___terrible	

1. Use the word *sports* in a sentence about television.

_____

2. Write a sentence that tells something you know about *basketball*.

_____

3. Write a sentence about school that includes the word *study*.

_____

4. Use the word *terrible* in a sentence about a game you played once.

_____

5. Write a sentence about a *disease* you know about.

_____

6. Use the word *popular* in a sentence about a TV show you like.

_____

7. Write a sentence about a bad winter that includes the word *freeze*.

_____

8. Use the word *guard* in a sentence about basketball.

_____

Measuring the Earth

SUMMARY This nonfiction reader describes some of the different devices used to measure various land forms. For example, the book explains how satellites are used to measure the heights of mountains and how sonar is used to measure the depths of the oceans.

LESSON VOCABULARY

average	depth
deserts	erupted
outrun	peak
tides	waterfalls

INTRODUCE THE BOOK

INTRODUCE THE TITLE AND AUTHOR Discuss with students the title and the author of *Measuring the Earth*. Based on the picture on the cover, have students suggest what types of land they think the book will be about. Then invite students to make educated guesses about what the title means.

BUILD BACKGROUND Have students brainstorm answers to the following questions:
How do you think people measure the height of mountains? How do you think people measure the depth of the ocean? *(Responses will vary.)* Explain that *Measuring the Earth* is a book about how people measure land forms. Have students suggest other questions they have about measuring features of Earth's surface.

PREVIEW/USE TEXT FEATURES Tell students to look through the book, paying special attention to the section headings. Ask: What types of land forms and measurements does this book talk about? *(heights of mountains, depths of oceans, directions, earthquakes, minerals)*

READ THE BOOK

SET PURPOSE Remind students that usually the main purpose of a nonfiction text is to inform the reader about a topic. Have students think about the headings in the book and set a purpose for reading by completing the following statement: *I would like to read this book to learn more about _____.*

STRATEGY SUPPORT: IMPORTANT IDEAS Tell students that when they read, it helps to locate the important ideas in a story. Remind students that an author can organize text in a story so that the important ideas are easier to find through text structures or signal words and phrases. Ask students to look at how the text is organized as they read. *(by description and text structure)*

COMPREHENSION QUESTIONS

PAGE 5 Is the height of Mount Everest a fact or an opinion? How do you know? *(fact; it can be proved true or false)*

PAGE 7 What question could you ask that is answered on this page? *(Possible response: How do scientists measure the depth of the ocean?)*

PAGE 11 How do scientists find the exact location of an earthquake? *(measure the earthquake's distance from three cities that use seismographs)*

PAGES 12–13 Use the Mohs scale to compare and contrast quartz and topaz. How are these minerals alike? How are they different? *(Possible responses: They are alike because they are both harder than feldspar; they are different because quartz is softer than topaz.)*

REVISIT THE BOOK

READER RESPONSE

1. Possible response: It shows how hard minerals are in relation to other minerals.
2. Possible response: I learned how to measure the depth of the ocean. This can help with underwater explorations.
3. page 8: *outrun*; page 9: *waterfalls*
4. Responses will vary but might include the Internet, an encyclopedia, or nonfiction reference book.

EXTEND UNDERSTANDING Remind students that when they *compare* two or more things, they are describing how those things are alike. When they *contrast* those things, they are talking only about how they are different. Have students choose two measuring devices from the book to compare and contrast. Then have students think about how these devices are alike and different.

ELL Help students complete a Venn diagram to compare two of the measuring devices in the book.

RESPONSE OPTIONS

WRITING Invite students to think of another measuring device that people use, such as a thermometer, scale, ruler, or measuring cup. Have students write a paragraph in which they compare and contrast their measuring device with one of the devices in the selection. Remind students to think of all the features that the two devices have in common and the features that are different.

SCIENCE CONNECTION

Provide groups of students with topographical maps of places around the world. Have each group think of five questions to ask other groups about their maps. Then have students exchange maps and try to answer another group's questions. Remind each group that it needs to provide answers to its questions.

Skill Work

TEACH/REVIEW VOCABULARY

Read through the Glossary with students. Pair students for a game called "10 Tries." Have one student draw on a piece of paper the number of blanks that correspond to letters in one of the vocabulary words and write the definition beneath the blanks. The partner tries to guess the word by guessing letters. The goal is to guess the word before 10 tries are exhausted. Partners should take turns choosing a word and guessing.

TARGET SKILL AND STRATEGY

GRAPHIC SOURCES Point out that authors often use graphic sources, like charts, graphs, and maps, to help the reader understand information in the text. Review with students the graphic sources on pages 10, 11, and 12. Discuss with students how these graphics helped them understand how seismographs and the Mohs Scale work.

IMPORTANT IDEAS Remind students that authors have many important ideas in a story. Explain that understanding which ideas are important will help the students better understand the story and the authors purpose for writing.

ADDITIONAL SKILL INSTRUCTION

FACT AND OPINION Review with students that *facts* are statements that can be proved true or false, while *opinions* are statements that tell someone's feelings or ideas about something. Discuss with students ways that facts may be proved true or false (checking in books, observing, asking experts). Point out some clue words that often indicate opinions, such as *best, worst, most, always, should.* Invite students to look for examples of one fact and one opinion as they read.

Graphic Sources

- **Graphic sources** are tools that present information visually.
- Charts, graphs, diagrams, maps, and pictures with captions are examples of **graphics sources**.

Directions Look back at the graphic sources in *Measuring the Earth* and answer the questions below.

1. Look at the illustration on page 10. Where do many earthquakes occur?

   _____

2. What does the chart on pages 12–13 tell you about the mineral gypsum?

   _____

3. Using the chart on pages 12–13, name two minerals that are harder than topaz.

   _____

4. **Directions** Create a bar graph that shows the heights of the following mountains:

Mount St. Helens	8,365 feet
Pike's Peak	14,115 feet
Mount Everest	29,035 feet

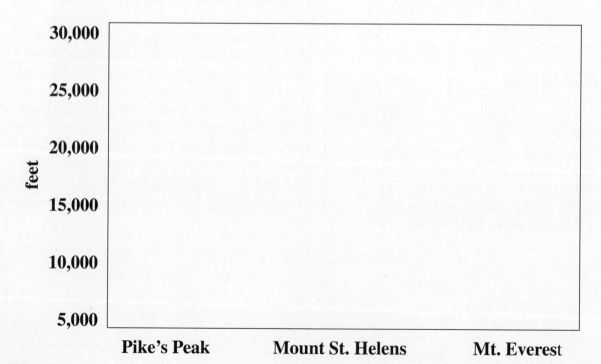

Name _____

Vocabulary

Directions Write the word from the word box that best matches each clue.

Check the Words You Know

___average	___depth	___deserts	___erupted
___outrun	___peak	___tides	___waterfalls

_____ **1.** streams of water that fall from high places

_____ **2.** places where many trees do not grow

_____ **3.** the highest place on a mountain

_____ **4.** the moon and the sun cause these

_____ **5.** to move faster than something else

_____ **6.** burst out violently

Directions Write the word or words from the box above that best fit each category.

7. Plural nouns _____

8. Verbs _____

9. Words about water _____

10. Words about measuring _____

11. Things that move _____

Fun with Hobbies and Science!

SUMMARY In *Fun with Hobbies and Science!*, the author introduces readers to a few of the ways in which some popular hobbies are related to science. This nonfiction reader describes how bird watching, learning about the past, and stargazing resemble the scientific fields of zoology, archeology, and astronomy. The author suggests how these hobbies could even lead to careers in science.

LESSON VOCABULARY

attic	board	chores
customers	labeled	spare
stamps		

INTRODUCE THE BOOK

INTRODUCE THE TITLE AND AUTHOR Discuss with students the title and the author of *Fun with Hobbies and Science!* Ask students what the boy in the cover photograph seems to be doing. (Possible response: looking at birds using binoculars) Discuss how this boy might be having "fun with science."

BUILD BACKGROUND Ask students to describe some of their own hobbies. Tell students that the selection they are about to read will describe some hobbies and how they are related to science.

ELL Have students talk about some hobbies or things people do in their spare time in their home countries. Suggest that students give examples of hobbies that are typical of their home countries but are uncommon in the United States.

PREVIEW/USE TEXT FEATURES Have students look through the book, focusing particularly on the headings. Discuss what sciences are mentioned in the headings. Invite students to talk about what the young people in the photographs appear to be doing and whether their activities look like any of the hobbies students mentioned in Build Background.

READ THE BOOK

SET PURPOSE Have students think of something they would like to know about a hobby and how it relates to science. Direct students to set one of the things they want to know about hobbies as their purpose for reading.

STRATEGY SUPPORT: INFERRING Remind students that *inferring* is combining prior knowledge with information from the text to create new information. Discuss with students what they know about hobbies. Ask students to keep this knowledge in mind while they read.

COMPREHENSION QUESTIONS

PAGE 5 Find a generalization that the author makes. (Possible responses: They come in many different shapes, sizes, and colors; some hummingbirds are only two inches long!)

PAGE 6 What do you know about birds that helps you understand the information? (Possible response: I already know that birds are afraid of people and fly away from them.)

PAGES 8–9 Find a generalization the author makes on these pages. (Possible responses: Old and ancient items are found every day in many different places; people sometimes like to save old items.)

PAGES 10–11 Use the text and captions on this page to help you draw a conclusion about where treasures from the past may be found. (Possible response: Treasures from the past may be found almost anywhere people live.)

PAGE 13 Make your own generalization about telescopes. (Possible response: Telescopes of any size are good tools for studying the stars.)

REVISIT THE BOOK

READER RESPONSE

1. Telescopes are made up of lenses, mirrors, or both. It is a fact because I can take apart a telescope to find the parts. Or I can look up the information in the encyclopedia.
2. Possible response: I can infer that many hobbies could lead to careers in science fields.
3. Chores, customers, stamps; sentences will vary.
4. about two inches; up to eight feet

EXTEND UNDERSTANDING

Once students have finished reading the selection, have them fill in the L column in KWL charts they should make. Invite volunteers to share some of the items in their Want to Know and Learned columns. Then have students add a fourth column entitled Still Want to Know. Tell students to fill in things they would still like to find out about science-related hobbies. Invite volunteers to share items from their S columns, and discuss as a class where students might look for more information.

RESPONSE OPTIONS

WRITING Have students write a paragraph describing a favorite hobby. Tell them to include in their paragraphs the materials and activities involved in the hobby and a sentence explaining why they enjoy the hobby in their spare time.

SCIENCE CONNECTION

TIME FOR Science

Provide students with a list and brief descriptions of some scientific fields, such as physics, chemistry, biology, and ecology. Have students put their hobbies in concept webs or charts and write the different ways their hobbies relate to science. Provide some examples, such as how stamp collecting can tell a person something about the past and how baseball uses physics. Have students share their webs or charts with the class.

Skill Work

TEACH/REVIEW VOCABULARY

Read through the Glossary with students. Have students work in small groups to write a paragraph about what some people like to do in their spare time. Tell them to use each of the vocabulary words at least once in their paragraphs. Invite groups to share their paragraphs with the class.

TARGET SKILL AND STRATEGY

FACT AND OPINION Review with students that a statement of *fact* can be proved true of false; and a statement of *opinion* is someone's viewpoint. Model by saying: If an elephant was sick, you would call a zoologist. I can prove this is a fact because zoologist work with large animals. Ask students write their own statements of fact and statements of opinion about a topic of their choice.

INFERRING After reading, discuss what was read with students. Ask students to use the information they learned while reading and combine it with what they already know to infer new information. Tell students that this will help them understand the ideas and topics of the story.

ADDITIONAL SKILL INSTRUCTION

DRAW CONCLUSIONS Point out that when readers make decisions about the facts in a book, they are *drawing conclusions*. As they read, have students think about the facts related to one of the hobbies in the selection. Tell students to use these facts to draw a conclusion about one of the hobbies discussed in the book.

Name _____

Fact and Opinion

- **Facts** can be proved true and false.
- **Opinions** are statements of ideas and feelings. They cannot be proved.

Directions Read the following sentences. Write whether each one is a fact or an opinion.

1. Some hobbies can take you outside while others may involve friends or adults. _____

2. Watching birds and other animals is important. _____

3. It is fun to find old treasures from the past. _____

4. Archaeology and stargazing are hobbies that relate to science. _____

5. Science is part of our daily lives. _____

There are many popular science hobbies out there. If you love animals, you can help take care of them. Caring for animals can be an interesting hobby. What you learn about animals now, may help you become a veterinarian in the future! A veterinarian is a doctor who takes care of animals. Veterinarians can have tough jobs.

Directions Read the following paragraph. Then write two facts and two opinions on the lines below.

6. _____

_____

7. _____

_____

8. _____

_____

9. _____

Vocabulary

Directions Use each of the following words in a sentence about hobbies.

Check the Words You Know

___attic   ___board   ___chores   ___stamps
___customers   ___labeled   ___spare

1. chores _____

2. labeled _____

3. attic _____

4. stamps _____

5. board _____

6. customers _____

7. spare _____

Directions Put each group of words in alphabetical order.

8. customers, stamps, chores, spare _____

9. labeled, attic, customers, board _____

10. spare, chores, labeled, hobby _____

11. telescope, attic, spare, binoculars _____

Great Women in U.S. History

SUMMARY This nonfiction reader provides brief biographies of three women who broke down barriers against their gender in the early twentieth century: Babe Didrikson Zaharias, Amelia Earhart, and Eleanor Roosevelt.

LESSON VOCABULARY

celebrate	continued
current	drowned
medal	stirred
strokes	

INTRODUCE THE BOOK

INTRODUCE THE TITLE AND AUTHOR Discuss the title and the author of *Great Women in U.S. History*. Point out that this is a biography. Discuss with students what a biography is, and have them predict who this biography is about, based on the cover illustration.

BUILD BACKGROUND Discuss with students some of the activities that their mothers, grandmothers, and aunts perform in their daily lives, including work outside the house. Then have girls in the class describe some of the things they like to do outside of school and what they plan to do in the future. Have boys in the class tell what their sisters, female cousins, or female friends do in their spare time. Ask students if girls can do the same things as boys do. Point out that not long ago, society believed there were certain things women should not do, such as vote.

ELL Have students describe the social roles of women in their home countries and compare them to women's roles in the United States.

PREVIEW/USE TEXT FEATURES Have students skim through the book and describe some of the activities the women are doing in the pictures. Invite students to make predictions about what types of women are featured in this biography.

READ THE BOOK

SET PURPOSE Turn to page 3 of the reader, and read together with students the names of the women who are featured in the book. Guide students to set their own purposes for reading by having them decide which woman they would like to learn more about.

STRATEGY SUPPORT: QUESTIONING Tell students to ask themselves questions as they read. This will help them focus on what they are reading. Then have students answer the questions that they posed earlier. When they finish reading, ask students if they have more questions. Suggest that they write down their new questions and research the answers.

COMPREHENSION QUESTIONS

PAGES 4–5 Name one statement of fact and one statement of opinion you see on these pages. How do you know which is which? *(Possible responses: Fact: Babe Didrikson Zaharias was born in Texas in 1911. Opinion: She knew she was just as strong as any boy. The fact can be checked in a book. The opinion is just Babe's belief about herself.)*

PAGE 9 What is the main idea of this page? *(Possible response: Amelia Earhart proved that women could do daring things.)*

PAGE 11 Did you find anything confusing on this page? How did you fix up your understanding? *(Possible response: I didn't know what polio was. I read on and found that Eleanor became Franklin's nurse and saw in the picture that he couldn't walk. I guessed that polio is a disease.)*

PAGE 13 After reading this page, what do you think is the main idea of this book? *(Possible response: There are great women in history who worked hard to gain respect for all women.)*

REVISIT THE BOOK

READER RESPONSE

1. Possible responses: Fact: She was born on July 24, 1897, in Kansas. I can check an encyclopedia. Opinion: Most people didn't think that women should fly planes. This is a statement of the a belief.
2. Responses will vary but should include a question followed by a strategy, such as read on, to answer the question.
3. *Current:* a flow of water. The current pulled our boat upstream. *Strokes:* acts of striking. It took three strokes of the hammer to drive in the nail.
4. I think Amelia Earhart was the most daring because she flew across an ocean alone.

EXTEND UNDERSTANDING Point out to students that biographies are often about exceptional people, or people who have done exceptional things. Explain to students that authors may use adjectives in their biographies to express to the reader just how important the subject is. Have students look through the book for adjectives that the author uses to describe the women in this biography. Discuss how the adjectives help the reader appreciate the accomplishments of these women.

RESPONSE OPTIONS

WRITING Have students write brief biographies of people whom they consider important in their lives, such as a relative, teacher, or coach. Remind students to use main ideas and supporting details to describe their subjects, as well as statements of fact and opinion.

SOCIAL STUDIES CONNECTION

Have students research other important women in history. Tell students to write reports and include information about each person's childhood, special obstacles, and accomplishments. Remind students to include paragraphs about why these women are important to remember.

Skill Work

TEACH/REVIEW VOCABULARY

Write the vocabulary words on the chalkboard. Form groups, and assign one word to each. Have each group find its word in the book. Tell students to create word webs for their words based on context clues in the book. Have groups share their webs and check their definitions against the Glossary.

TARGET SKILL AND STRATEGY

FACT AND OPINION Explain to students that a *statement of fact* is a statement that can be proved true or false. A *statement of opinion* is a person's beliefs or ideas about something. Remind students that they just need to know that the statement *can* be checked by looking in reference sources, by asking an expert, or by observing. Give examples of statements of facts and opinions, and discuss with students how to distinguish each. Then tell students to list one statement of fact and one statement of opinion for each of the three women profiled in the reader.

QUESTIONING Review with students that asking *questions* is a way to further understand a topic and gain more information. Ask students what questions they had about the story. Have students write down their questions; as they read they can see whether their questions are answered. If not, direct them to additional resources to complete their inquiry.

ADDITIONAL SKILL INSTRUCTION

MAIN IDEA AND DETAILS Review with students that the *main idea* is the most important idea about a topic of a passage or a selection. Supporting *details* are the smaller pieces of information about the main idea. Tell students to look for the main idea about each woman in the reader and find two details that support this idea.

Name _____

Fact and Opinion

- A **statement of fact** is a statement that can be proved true or false. You can check a statement of fact by looking in reference sources, asking an expert, or observing.

- A **statement of opinion** is a person's beliefs or ideas about something. You cannot prove whether it is true or false.

Directions Read the following passage. Then answer the questions below.

In 1932, Babe went to the Olympic Games in Los Angeles. She set a world record in the javelin throw. Newspapers called her the "World's Greatest Athlete." Babe knew she could do anything she could put her mind to.

Next, Babe took up golfing. Her golf strokes were so strong that she became a champion at that too. In 1950, she was named the Outstanding Woman Athlete of the Half-Century. She died of cancer at a young age, but her memory and courage will live forever.

1. What is one statement of fact that the author makes in this passage?

_____

2. Where could you check whether the statement is true or false?

_____

3. What is one statement of opinion that the author makes in this passage?

_____

4. How do you know that this is a statement of opinion?

_____

_____

5. Which sentence in this passage contains both a statement of fact and a statement of opinion? Which part is which?

_____

_____

_____

Vocabulary

Directions Choose the word from the box that best matches each definition. Write the letters of the word on the lines.

Check the Words You Know
___celebrate ___continued ___current ___drowned
___medal ___stirred ___strokes

1. awakened or brought to the surface __ __ __ __ __ __ __
                                                                1   2

2. to make known or famous __ __ __ __ __ __ __ __
                               3

3. a small piece of metal, usually with a special design, given as an award for some outstanding act __ __ __ __ __
                           4

4. went on in some action __ __ __ __ __ __ __ __ __
                                   5

5. in tennis, golf, etc., several strikings of the ball __ __ __ __ __ __ __
                                   6

6. died by suffocation in water __ __ __ __ __ __ __
                           7

Directions Write down the letters from the numbered spaces above. Then unscramble the letters to form a word from the box. Use the word to answer the riddle below.

What word describes an event that is happening today?

7. _____

Directions Write sentences as directed below.

8. Use the word *stirred* in a sentence about cooking.

_____

_____

9. Use the word *celebrate* in a sentence about your favorite holiday.

_____

_____

Buddy Ran Away

SUMMARY This is a fictional story about a dog finding its way home over a great distance by using natural instincts and a keen sense of smell.

LESSON VOCABULARY

clutched	echoed
gully	reeds
scrambled	thatch
valley	

INTRODUCE THE BOOK

INTRODUCE THE TITLE AND AUTHOR Discuss with students the title and author of *Buddy Ran Away*. Ask students what the title makes them imagine the story is about. Direct students' attention to the cover illustration and ask students how the illustration adds to the information the title gives them.

BUILD BACKGROUND Ask students if they have ever had a pet that got lost or if they have ever known anyone who had a pet that got lost. Discuss how the owner of the pet felt and what he or she did to get the pet back. Ask students if they have ever noticed the way dogs always sniff the ground, which can lead to a discussion of dogs' excellent sense of smell.

PREVIEW/USE TEXT FEATURES Suggest that students look at all the illustrations in the story. Ask students what the illustrations make them imagine the story is about. Direct students' attention to the drawings on page 7 and on page 15 and ask them how the expression on the character's face gives them clues as to what is happening in the story.

READ THE BOOK

SET PURPOSE Have students set a purpose for reading *Buddy Ran Away*. Students' curiosity and interest in dogs and their natural instincts should guide this purpose.

STRATEGY SUPPORT: MONITOR AND CLARIFY Explain to students that it is important to monitor, or keep an eye on, their understanding of what they are reading. Tell students that there are different ways to clarify a comprehension problem. Suggest that students take notes about what is happening in the story. Then they can track the story and check their notes to see if the story makes sense. Also tell students that if they are asked a question about the story, they can reread to review information they may have forgotten.

COMPREHENSION QUESTIONS

PAGE 3 Even though this is the beginning of the story, there is also an ending on this page. What is it? *(It is the end of Sam's vacation with Alan and Alan's family.)*

PAGES 8–11 Using a graphic organizer, list what things Sam did to try and find Buddy. *(He called for him, he put up a notice, he left small pieces of his clothing for Buddy to find the scent.)*

PAGE 14 Why was Sam hopeful after he read about beagles? *(He learned that beagles were very good at following a scent.)*

PAGE 15 Were you surprised by the ending of the story? Why or why not? *(Possible response: I was surprised because I thought the dog was really lost. I was not surprised because I learned beagles could follow scents, and Sam had thrown out pieces of his clothes so Buddy could follow the scent.)*

REVISIT THE BOOK

READER RESPONSE

1. Possible responses: Cause: Rabbit is startled; Effect: Rabbit runs out of grass. Cause: Rabbit runs out of grass; Effect: Buddy chases the rabbit. Cause: Buddy chases the rabbit; Effect: Buddy gets lost.
2. Possible response: underbrush I used the illustrations and read on.
3. Students should include *valley, reeds, gully,* and *echoed* in their descriptions.
4. Possible response: I have a dog. Some pets can run and play.

EXTEND UNDERSTANDING Remind students that the character is the person who talks and does the action in a story. Discuss the character of Sam with students. Have students reread pages 3–9 in the book *Buddy Ran Away,* and then ask: What do we know about Sam? What clues in the story tell us what Sam is like? Have students identify character traits and cite "proof" from the story. Then ask: Based on what you know about Sam, what do you think he will do next in the story? Why do you think so?

RESPONSE OPTIONS

WRITING Ask students to imagine they are Sam and to create a commercial asking Buddy to come home. Students can also design a "LOST" poster if they are interested.

SCIENCE CONNECTION

Invite students to research another dog with a strong sense of smell, such as a bloodhound, and ask them to write and illustrate a report on that breed.

Skill Work

TEACH/REVIEW VOCABULARY

Review vocabulary words with students. Then write out the words with some of the letters missing and invite students to name the vocabulary word. Do this with all the vocabulary words, and then have students use each word in a sentence.

ELL Review vocabulary words with students. Personalize each word by asking them questions such as, "If I were in a valley, where would I be?" Do the same for the remaining vocabulary words.

TARGET SKILL AND STRATEGY

CAUSE AND EFFECT Point out to students that an *effect* is what happened and a *cause* is why it happened. Students might look for the clue words *because* and *so.* Remind students that an author might not use clue words to identify a cause-and-effect relationship. Ask students to look for two examples of cause and effect in the story.

MONITOR AND CLARIFY Remind students that when they ask questions about a text, they help themselves better understand and remember what they read. Tell students that sometimes we need to pause to ask ourselves if we have understood what we have read so far. If we feel confused, we can look for details that help us understand what we're reading.

ADDITIONAL SKILL INSTRUCTION

SEQUENCE Remind students that sequence of events is the order in which things happen in a story. Sometimes clue words such as *first, then,* or *finally* help identify the sequence. Invite students to make a time line of events in a story they know. Then ask them to use a time line to map out sequence as they read *Buddy Ran Away.*

Cause and Effect

- A **cause** is why something happened.
- An **effect** is what happened.

Directions Read each of the following effects in *Buddy Ran Away*. For each effect, write the cause.

1. The Rabbit runs out of the grass.

Cause: _____

_____

2. Buddy chases the rabbit.

Cause: _____

_____

3. Buddy gets lost.

Cause: _____

_____

4. Sam searches for Buddy.

Cause: _____

_____

5. Buddy found his way home.

Cause: _____

_____

Vocabulary

Directions Find the vocabulary words from the box hidden in the word search below. Look up, down, and across.

Check the Words You Know

___clutched   ___gully   ___scrambled   ___valley

___echoed   ___reeds   ___thatch

```
Q  E  H  L  J  S  N  R  V
A  C  L  U  T  C  H  E  D
M  H  B  Y  I  R  L  E  P
F  O  K  H  N  A  Q  D  O
G  E  Q  C  I  M  X  S  Z
R  D  L  T  F  B  G  H  C
B  C  V  A  L  L  E  Y  Q
N  A  X  H  R  E  Q  S  N
J  V  M  T  K  D  O  L  C
O  K  G  U  L  L  Y  X  V
```

Directions Use each word below in a sentence.

gully   scrambled   clutched   valley

1. _____

_____

2. _____

_____

3. _____

_____

4. _____

_____

Cowboy Slim's Dude Ranch

SUMMARY In this fictional story, a young boy vacations at a dude ranch with his parents. Students learn about how where we are and what we do affects the clothing we wear.

LESSON VOCABULARY

cotton	festival
graceful	handkerchief
pace	pale
rhythm	snug

INTRODUCE THE BOOK

INTRODUCE THE TITLE AND AUTHOR Discuss with students the title and author of *Cowboy Slim's Dude Ranch*. Have students look at the cover art. Ask: What is the boy doing? What do you think this story will be about?

BUILD BACKGROUND Ask students if they have ever gone to a ranch or horseback riding. Ask student to discuss how vacationing at a dude ranch might be different from other vacations. Talk about working vacations, where visitors do chores, ride horses, and participate in work activities.

PREVIEW/TAKE A PICTURE WALK As students preview the book, encourage them to look closely at the illustrations and ask what information about the story these illustrations provide. Encourage students to look for details that indicate the setting. They should think about how the setting might influence a character's actions.

READ THE BOOK

SET PURPOSE Have students set a purpose for reading *Cowboy Slim's Dude Ranch*. Have students think about something that they might like to know about a dude ranch. This should guide their purpose for reading.

STRATEGY SUPPORT: VISUALIZE Explain to students that to *visualize* is to form a picture in their minds about what is happening in the story. Tell students that forming pictures in their minds will help them understand and what they are reading. Model using page 3. Say: After reading this page, I can picture Dad walking in the front door in a suit with a red bandana around his neck, a large white cowboy hat on, and a huge grin across his face.

COMPREHENSION QUESTIONS

PAGE 5 Why does Danny guess that his parents are dressed for a costume party? *(Danny thinks that they look completely ridiculous in their cowhand outfits.)*

PAGE 9 What does Danny notice about cowboy Slim when he first meets him? *(Danny notices that he is smiling and friendly. He is also slim, but muscular and tan from his work on the ranch.)* What does he notice about Cowboy Slim's clothing? *(Danny admires Cowboy Slim's leather boots and wide hat.)*

PAGE 11 Why do cowhands wear a hat and handkerchief? *(Cowhands wear a hat to shade their faces from the sun. They use a handkerchief to wipe the sweat from their faces.)*

PAGE 15 How does Danny's attitude change at the end of the story? *(Danny now wants to wear the cowboy clothing because he thinks it is cool to be a cowboy. He also learned that there is a purpose for each piece of cowboy clothing.)*

REVISIT THE BOOK

READER RESPONSE

1. Possible responses: Home—jeans, tee-shirt, sneakers
Ranch—long-sleeved shirt, hat, leather boots
Both: socks, underwear, jeans

2. Possible response: I visualized lots of miles of lonely road, not too many people or animals.

3. tight fitting

4. Possible responses: Danny learns that what cowhands wear has a purpose. At the end of the story, he is excited to wear the cowboy clothes and wants to show his friends.

EXTEND UNDERSTANDING As students read the story, ask them to pay close attention to what the dude ranch looks like in the illustrations. Discuss how the illustrations help tell the story.

RESPONSE OPTIONS

WRITING Bring in examples of cowboy clothing from newspapers or magazines. Discuss this clothing with students, and then ask them to write an advertisement for one of the articles of clothing. Remind students to include details they learned from *Cowboy Slim's Dude Ranch.*

SOCIAL STUDIES CONNECTION

Time For SOCIAL STUDIES

Suggest that students research what cowhands and ranchers wear and why they wear it. Then have them write a report they can share with the class.

Skill Work

TEACH/REVIEW VOCABULARY

Read aloud the vocabulary words. Ask students about words they may already know and explain words that are not familiar. Have students use each vocabulary word in a sentence.

ELL Find pictures of items commonly used on a ranch, such as cowboy hat, saddle, cabin, horses, cattle, campfire, and lantern. Help English language learners identify and label these items. Say the word as you label the item, and ask students to repeat the word.

TARGET SKILL AND STRATEGY

COMPARE AND CONTRAST Share with students that a *comparison* tells how two or more things are alike, and a *contrast* shows how two or more things are different. As they read, tell students to ask questions such as, *How are the ranch and Danny's home similar?* and *How are Danny and Cowboy Slim different?*

VISUALIZE Remind students that visualizing can help them better understand and remember the story. Tell students, if they are having trouble visualizing a picture, certain words or phrases can help them form a picture in their mind. Ask students to share what pictures they saw in their minds as you read.

ADDITIONAL SKILL INSTRUCTION

MAIN IDEA Remind students that the main idea tells what a story is mostly about. The details are pieces of information that support the main idea. Ask students to identify the main idea and details as they read this story.

Compare and Contrast

- When you **compare** two or more things, you think about how they are alike and how they are different.
- When you **contrast** two or more things, you only think about how they are different.

Directions Look back at the selection *Cowboy Slim's Dude Ranch*. Compare and contrast the life on a dude ranch and life at home.

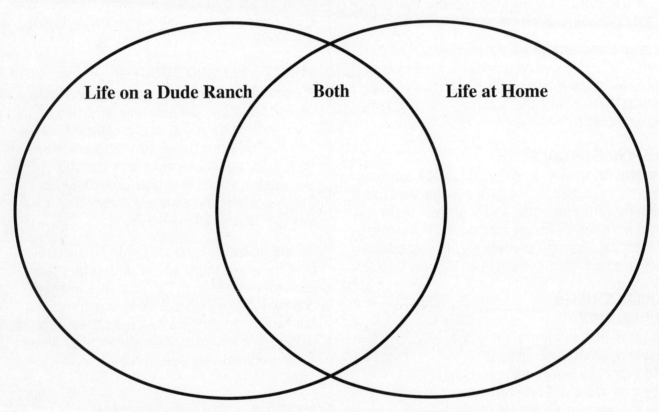

Life on a Dude Ranch   **Both**   **Life at Home**

1. How is life on a dude ranch similar to your life at home?

_____

_____

2. How is life on a dude ranch different to your life at home?

_____

_____

Vocabulary

Directions Fill in the crossword puzzle using the clues and the words in the box.

Check the Words You Know

___cotton	___festival	___graceful	___handkerchief
___pace	___pale	___rhythm	___snug

Across

3. soft square of cloth

5. a step

6. cloth made from white plant fibers

7. fitting closely

8. not bright

Down

1. a strong beat in music or poetry

2. beautiful in form or movement

4. an entertainment

Celebrate Around the World

SUMMARY This nonfiction reader describes special celebrations from around the world in many different countries and cultures. The book also discusses several American celebrations, such as Thanksgiving and Independence Day.

LESSON VOCABULARY

bouquets	circus
difficult	nibbling
pier	soar
swallow	

INTRODUCE THE BOOK

INTRODUCE THE TITLE AND AUTHOR Discuss with students the title and author of *Celebrate Around the World.* Have students look at the cover art. Ask: What are these pictures of? What do you think this book will be about?

BUILD BACKGROUND Discuss with students the special celebrations they have taken part in and enjoyed. What special celebrations do they have with their families that commemorate their culture and family traditions?

PREVIEW/TAKE A PICTURE WALK As students preview the book, encourage them to look closely at the photographs and ask what information these pictures provide. Point out the expressions on the peoples' faces, and ask students how this helps them understand what might be going on during the celebration.

READ THE BOOK

SET PURPOSE Have students set a purpose for reading *Celebrate Around the World.* Students' interest and curiosity about celebrations of different countries and cultures can guide this purpose. As students read, suggest that they take notes about questions they have about different holidays.

STRATEGY SUPPORT: INFERRING Before reading, ask students to think about what they know about holidays. Tell students to keep their prior knowledge in mind as they read. After reading, ask student to combine their prior knowledge with the new information they have read to learn something new.

COMPREHENSION QUESTIONS

PAGE 3 Why are celebrations like the ones pictured important? *(Holidays are important because they are times when families, friends, and communities come together to share good times.)*

PAGES 6–9 Why do so many traditions and celebration use lights? *(Responses will vary, but lights often symbolize the end of winter or bringing light into the world.)*

PAGES 16–17 What is the old story of the Chinese New Year celebration based on? *(People were frightened of a beast that appeared at the end of winter. They learned that the beast was afraid of birth lights, loud noises, and the color red.)*

PAGE 18 In what other Chinese celebration is the dragon used and for what purpose? *(The dragon is used in the annual Chinese Dragon Boat Festival to keep away evil spirits that might cause illness.)*

REVISIT THE BOOK

READER RESPONSE

1. Holidays around the world. Details will vary but should support the main idea.
2. Possible response: I know candles are used for many holidays. I read they symbolize different things. I can infer candles are an important part of many holidays.
3. Possible response: Did you swallow too much water?
4. Responses will vary but should include two holidays and how they are alike and different.

EXTEND UNDERSTANDING As students read the story, ask them to pay close attention to the different ways people celebrate and use lights in celebrations. Afterward, discuss their thoughts about lights and what they mean.

RESPONSE OPTIONS

WRITING Ask students to write about other ways they or their families celebrate special days. Perhaps they celebrate the Fourth of July or family members' birthdays in a special way with their family.

SOCIAL STUDIES CONNECTION

Invite students to do more research about celebrations. Have them work as a class to make a *Celebrations Around the World* scrapbook. Students can record recipes, songs, and activities in the book to create the perfect celebration source book.

Skill Work

TEACH/REVIEW VOCABULARY

Review the vocabulary words with students. Then play Vocabulary Master with students. Give students three different definitions for each vocabulary word, including one that is silly. Have students guess the correct definition.

ELL Find pictures of items commonly used for celebrations, such as birthday candles, piñatas, streamers, balloons, and so on. Help English language learners identify and label these items. Say the word as you label each item, and ask students to repeat the word.

TARGET SKILL AND STRATEGY

MAIN IDEA AND DETAILS Share with students that the *main idea* is the most important idea about a topic in a passage or selection. Supporting *details* are the smaller pieces of information about the main idea. As students read, ask them to look for the main idea of this selection and supporting details.

INFERRING Remind students that *inferring* is using information that is already known and combining it with what they have read to create new information. Model using page 4. Say: I know piñatas are fun. I read that they are used to celebrate Cinco de Mayo. I can infer that the reason for celebrating on Cinco de Mayo is for a joyous cause.

ADDITIONAL SKILL INSTRUCTION

COMPARE AND CONTRAST Remind students that when we *compare*, we look at how things are similar; when we *contrast*, we look at how things are different. As students read the book *Celebrate Around the World*, have them notice similarities and differences in how different countries and cultures celebrate holidays.

Main Idea and Details

- The **main idea** is the author's most important point about a topic.
- Sometimes the main idea is not stated directly in a selection, but the details of a selection can give you clues.

Directions Read the following passages. Then write down the main idea and list two details from the passage that support your answer.

> Jewish people celebrate the Festival of Lights, or Hanukkah. The holiday lasts for eight nights to symbolize the eight nights that the oil lamp burned. Jewish families light the candles on the menorah, a candleholder with nine candles. Each night, one candle is used to light the other eight.

1. Main idea: _____

_____

2. Supporting detail: _____

_____

3. Supporting detail: _____

_____

> Holidays are a time for families to come together. One example is Children's Day. It is celebrated in Japan on May 5. Families fly streamers shaped as paper fish. The fish stand for courage and strength. Children nibble on their favorite foods and watch kites soar in the air.

4. Main idea: _____

_____

5. Supporting detail: _____

_____

6. Supporting detail: _____

_____

Vocabulary

Directions Fill in the blank with the word from the word box that matches the definition.

> ## Check the Words You Know
>
> ___bouquets   ___circus   ___difficult   ___nibbling
> ___pier   ___soar   ___swallow

_____ **1.** *n.* a group of traveling entertainers including clowns and acrobats

_____ **2.** *n.* bunches of cut flowers that have been specially chosen or arranged

_____ **3.** *adj.* not easy

_____ **4.** *v.* to fly at great heights

_____ **5.** *n.* a boat dock

_____ **6.** *v.* to take into the stomach through the throat

_____ **7.** *v.* taking small quick bites of something

Directions Write a short paragraph discussing one of the holidays described in *Celebrate Around the World.* Use as many vocabulary words as possible.

_____

_____

_____

_____

_____

_____

_____

Joanie's House Becomes a Home

SUMMARY Joanie is not happy when she learns that her family is moving from San Francisco to Boston. She doesn't want to leave her friends and all her things. When the movers arrive with all the belongings from their house in San Francisco, however, the new house in Boston starts to feel more like a home.

LESSON VOCABULARY

airport	cellar
curious	delicious
described	farewell
homesick	memories
raindrops	

INTRODUCE THE BOOK

INTRODUCE THE TITLE AND AUTHOR Discuss with students the title and the author of *Joanie's House Becomes a Home*. Ask them what they think the book will be about based on the title and the cover illustration. Ask students to talk about what makes a place feel like home.

BUILD BACKGROUND Invite students to share whether they have ever moved with their families. Ask: Where did you move from? Where did you move to? How did you feel when you found out your family was moving? Did you want to leave? Did you miss your old friends? How long did it take before your new home felt like a home?

PREVIEW Have students preview the book by looking at the illustrations and the section titles. In particular, have them notice the map on page 7 and the floorplan diagrams on pages 12, 14–15, and 16–17. Ask students to think about how these text features give an idea of what the book will be about.

READ THE BOOK

SET PURPOSE Have students set a purpose for reading *Joanie's House Becomes a Home*. Students' interest in families that move and in making new friends should guide this purpose.

STRATEGY SUPPORT: MONITOR AND FIX UP Have students use a graphic organizer to track what happens in the story. They may wish to use a time line or a sequence-of-events graphic organizer. Have students note points at which they have questions about what happens and have them go back to the text to add to their understanding.

COMPREHENSION QUESTIONS

PAGE 6 How will the Chens get to Boston? How will their things get to Boston? (*take a plane; get driven in a truck by moving men*)

PAGE 8 How do the raindrops on the window of the plane make Joanie feel? (*sad*)

PAGE 11 What is the first thing Mrs. Chen does to make Joanie feel at home? (*gives her a plant*)

PAGE 12 What did Mrs. Chen use to describe the new house to Joanie? (*a floor plan*)

PAGE 18 What did Joanie's friends from San Francisco send her? (*a team picture with all their names signed*)

PAGE 19 What does Joanie's new friend, Kelly, like about Boston? (*the ice cream*)

REVIST THE BOOK

READER RESPONSE

1. 1) They packed all their things into boxes. 2) Moving men loaded the boxes and furniture into a truck. 3) The Chens took a plane to Boston.

2. Possible response: She's unhappy about moving.

3. Possible response: indifferent, uninterested, unconcerned

4. Possible response: Mr. and Mrs. Chen's room, Joanie's room, Jimmy's room, living room, dining room

EXTEND UNDERSTANDING Have students comment on the illustrations in the selection. Invite them to explain how they show changes in Joanie's feelings. Invite them to explain the changes in the floor plan from page 12 to pages 14–15 to pages 16–17.

RESPONSE OPTIONS

WRITING Invite students to write a paragraph about what it would be like to move to a new place with their families, or write about a time they moved. Have them tell how they felt before they moved and include when they felt like the new place was home.

SOCIAL STUDIES CONNECTION

Time For SOCIAL STUDIES

Students can learn more about how people feel when they move to a new home by going to the library or using the Internet. Have them look for stories about students who came to this country with their families as immigrants from other countries. Encourage them to think about how people gain things and lose things when they move to a new home.

Skill Work

TEACH/REVIEW VOCABULARY

Challenge students to write a short story that includes each of the vocabulary words. Have them read their stories to the class.

TARGET SKILL AND STRATEGY

SEQUENCE Remind students that *sequence* means "order." Explain that clue words such as *first, then,* and *finally* are often used to signal sequence. Invite them to look for these clue words as they read.

ELL Invite students to make a list of sequence clue words. Suggest they compare them with similar words in their home language. Have them use the words in English to retell the story. Encourage them to retell the events of the story in order.

MONITOR AND FIX UP Remind students that a good reader takes note when a text is making sense and when it has stopped making sense. A good reader also has strategies for restoring understanding. Challenge students to stop and ask themselves whether they understand the story every two pages. Have them keep track of what happens first, next, and last.

ADDITIONAL SKILL INSTRUCTION

DRAW CONCLUSIONS Remind students that a *conclusion* is a decision you reach that makes sense after you think about the details and the characters and what happens in a story. Ask them to consider whether the conclusions they draw make sense. If not, invite them to rethink their conclusions and draw new conclusions. Have them share their conclusions with the class and support them with details from the story.

Sequence

- **Sequence** is the order of events in a story.
- Authors sometimes use clue words such as **first, next, then,** and **last** to tell the order of events.

Directions Read the following paragraph based on *Joanie's House Becomes a Home*. Then put the following events in the correct sequence. Write the letters on the lines below.

The Chens said farewell to their old house in San Francisco, California. First, the Chens packed all their things into boxes. Second, moving men loaded the boxes and the furniture into a truck. Next, the Chens went to the airport and flew to Boston. Then they arrived at their new house. Finally, the moving men arrived with all their things.

a. The moving men arrived with all their things.

b. The Chens went to the airport and flew to Boston.

c. The moving men loaded the boxes and furniture into the truck.

d. The Chens packed all their things into boxes.

e. The Chens arrived at their new house.

1. _____

2. _____

3. _____

4. _____

5. _____

Name _____

Vocabulary

Directions Draw a line from each word to its definition.

Check the Words You Know

__airport	__cellar	__curious	__delicious
__described	__farewell	__homesick	__memories
__raindrops			

1. airport   missing friends and family

2. cellar   thoughts of things that happened in the past

3. curious   told about, explained

4. delicious   a place where airplanes take off and land

5. described   very tasty

6. farewell   drops of water falling from clouds

7. homesick   eager to find out about something

8. memories   an expression of good wishes when saying good-bye

9. raindrops   a room below ground in a house

Directions Write two sentences about a time when you had to say good-bye to someone. Use at least two of the vocabulary words.

10. _____

11. _____

Kapuapua's Magic Shell

SUMMARY This story is about a kind old Hawaiian man named Kapuapua who loves to sail the ocean in his canoe. One day, he comes upon an island where he hopes to get water and food. The islanders will give him water, but no food, so he tricks them by making seashell soup. The islanders want some of it, but Kapuapua will share only if they contribute food to it. This turns into a big feast.

LESSON VOCABULARY

bakery	batch
boils	braided
dough	ingredients
mixture	

INTRODUCE THE BOOK

INTRODUCE THE TITLE AND AUTHOR Discuss with students the title and author of *Kapuapua's Magic Shell*. Ask students what they think the book will be about. Does the illustration on the cover give any clues?

BUILD BACKGROUND Ask students if any of them have been to Hawaii. If so, have them talk about what they saw and the food they ate. If students have collected shells at the beach, have them describe this experience to the class.

PREVIEW Encourage students to look at all of the illustrations in the book. Do the illustrations give them an idea of what the story will be about?

READ THE BOOK

SET PURPOSE Have students *set a purpose* for reading *Kapuapua's Magic Shell*. Remind students that setting a purpose helps guide their reading. They could think about how Kapuapua will get what he wants in the story.

STRATEGY SUPPORT: SUMMARIZE Help students understand that summarizing what they read helps them organize what happens in a story. For instance, suggest that students take a section of *Kapuapua's Magic Shell*, such as pages 8 to 11. Have them summarize what Kapuapua does to get food from the villagers. Then suggest that they summarize how this idea grows into a big celebration.

COMPREHENSION QUESTIONS

PAGE 5 Why were the islanders at first so upset that Kapuapua had landed on their island? *(They did not want to share their food.)*

PAGE 8 What happened that gave Kapuapua his idea? *(A coconut fell on his head.)*

PAGE 11 What did the villagers have to do in order to taste the magic soup? *(They had to add some food to the soup.)*

PAGE 13 What did Kapuapua teach the islanders to bake? *(sweet bread)*

PAGE 16 Besides the bread and the soup, what other things did they eat at their feast? *(roasted pig and fruit)*

PAGE 19 Kapuapua was treated like a thief at the beginning of the story. How was he treated by the end? *(like a king)*

REVISIT THE BOOK

READER RESPONSE

1. Possible response: They were not very friendly. They didn't want to share their food.

2. Possible responses: There are many ways to achieve your goal. Instead of getting angry, get creative.

3. Summaries will vary.

4. Possible response: Beginning: They didn't want to share their food. Middle: They helped Kapuapua make his soup. End: They treated Kapuapua like a king.

EXTEND UNDERSTANDING Have students think more about the lesson of this story. What is the lesson that the islanders learned? What is the lesson that the author wants us to take away from the story?

RESPONSE OPTIONS

WRITING Have students imagine they have landed their canoe on a deserted island. What would they do to find food and water? How would they make a shelter?

SOCIAL STUDIES CONNECTION

Time For **SOCIAL STUDIES**

Have students research the islands of Hawaii. They should find out about its history, food, music, and dance. How did the original Hawaiians get there? What types of boats have Hawaiians used? Students can also look into the volcanic history of the islands.

Skill Work

TEACH/REVIEW VOCABULARY

Go over the meanings of the vocabulary words. Tell students to guess a mystery word based on three clues about the word. One set of students can make the clues, and another group can guess. Create clues for all other vocabulary words.

ELL Have students talk about a time they were invited to someone's home for dinner or a time when someone came to dinner at their home. Ask: What did you eat and who was at the table?

TARGET SKILL AND STRATEGY

DRAW CONCLUSIONS Remind students that *drawing conclusions* means making a decision after thinking about facts or details. Have students think about the following question as they read: Why does Kapuapua's trick work so well on the islanders? *(They are curious about the magic soup.)*

SUMMARIZE Remind students that *summarizing* is boiling down a story to its main points. To gain practice, have students summarize their favorite books or movies. Or they can take notes as they read this story and summarize it once they have finished reading the book. They should try to draw conclusions about the story's lesson.

ADDITIONAL SKILL INSTRUCTION

THEME Without using the word *theme*, remind students that many stories include one big idea, or lesson, about how people should act. Discuss the lessons in familiar stories such as *The Tortoise and the Hare (slow and steady wins the race)*. Ask students how that big idea provides a lesson about how people should behave.

Draw Conclusions

- To draw a **conclusion** is to think about facts and details and decide something about them.

Directions Read the following passage from *Kapuapua's Magic Shell*. Then fill in the chart below. Write a fact about Kapuapua in the first box. Write a fact about the villagers in the second box. Write your conclusion in the last box.

Kapuapua continued with the story. He told the villagers, "As soon as the water boils, I will make a pot of magic soup." But, he told them, they could not have any of his soup. There was only enough for one person.

Soon the villagers asked if they could add some food of their own. Then there would be enough for them to taste. Kapuapua just smiled and kept on stirring.

Kapuapua picked up the seashell. He was the only one who knew it was just a regular shell that he found a long time ago. He dropped it into the water. A little splash jumped from the pot and landed on the back of his hand. Then he said, "Mmm, this soup is going to be great!"

Soon the villagers begged for a taste. Kapuapua told them they could have a taste if they added other ingredients to the pot. They asked what they could add to the mixture.

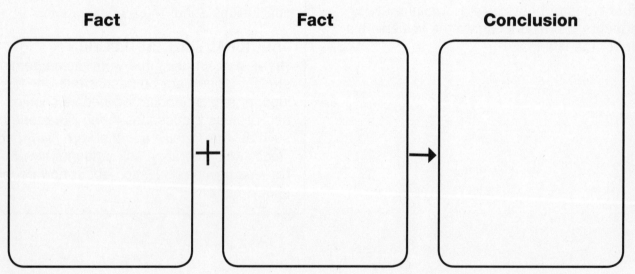

Fact	Fact	Conclusion
	+	→

Vocabulary

Directions Complete each sentence with the word from the word box that fits best.

Check the Words You Know

___bakery   ___batch   ___boils   ___braided
___dough   ___ingredients ___mixture

1. Kapuapua made a _____ of magic soup.

2. The villagers added fish and vegetables to the _____ in the pot.

3. Kapuapua was pleased with all the _____ the villagers brought.

4. We can buy wonderful bread from the _____ .

5. Kapuapua used to wear his long hair _____ .

6. When the water _____, Kapuapua throws the shell into the soup.

7. The baker added raisins and nuts to the bread _____ .

Directions Write a paragraph about all the food at Kapuapua's feast, using as many vocabulary words as possible.

_____

_____

_____

_____

_____

Bobby's New Apartment

SUMMARY This fictional reader tells the story of Bobby and his parents moving from a house in a small town to an apartment building in a big city. It shows how Bobby is scared at first, but then adjusts to his new life and home.

LESSON VOCABULARY

cardboard	feast
fierce	flights
pitcher	ruined
stoops	treasure

INTRODUCE THE BOOK

INTRODUCE THE TITLE AND AUTHOR Discuss with students the title and author of *Bobby's New Apartment*. Ask students to describe what they think the book will be about based on the title and the cover illustration. Ask students if they think Bobby's new apartment is in a big city or small town.

BUILD BACKGROUND Ask students if they have ever moved to a new place, and if so, how they felt about leaving their old home. Ask students to name some of the reasons that people move to new homes. Elicit some of the adjustments people have to make when they move to a new place.

ELL Ask students if their family has ever moved. If they answer yes, ask them to discuss the good and bad parts of their move. Ask all students to think about what they would pack for a move and what they would want to do before they left (example: say good-by to their friends).

PREVIEW Have students skim the reader, paying close attention to the illustrations. Ask students what they think the book is going to be about based on its illustrations.

READ THE BOOK

SET PURPOSE Encourage students to set a purpose for reading this book. After they preview the book and look at the illustrations, ask them to write down a few questions that they hope to answer by reading the book.

STRATEGY SUPPORT: PRIOR KNOWLEDGE Ask students to discuss what they know about the differences between living in a big city and living in a small town. Depending on the environment the students live in, ask the group if anyone has lived in the other kind of environment. If so, ask those students to explain what they had the hardest time adjusting to after they moved.

COMPREHENSION QUESTIONS

PAGE 4 What sentences on this page are clues to how Bobby is feeling? (*He looked a little fierce to Bobby. We don't even know anyone. Bobby missed his house and his friends already.*)

PAGE 4 Replace the word *fierce* on this page with another word with the same meaning. (*Possible responses: mean, scary, angry*)

PAGE 6 After the doorman, who are the next people Bobby meets in his new building? (*Hazel and Mrs. Low*)

PAGES 14–18 Name some of the reasons why Bobby decided he liked his new apartment. (*riding his bike in the basement; the playground on the roof; never feeling lonely*)

PAGE 17 What does Jose say that compares living in an apartment building to living in a small town? (*He says people in the building need to help each other.*)

REVISIT THE BOOK

READER RESPONSE

1. Possible response: to show that moving can be difficult; to show that apartment life can be interesting and fun
2. Possible response: House: only one family. Both: People help each other. Apartment: many families in one building
3. Possible responses: to mean "great," to describe a comic-book hero
4. Possible responses: He shows Bobby that people in the building are nice. He becomes Bobby's friend. He shows him around the building.

EXTEND UNDERSTANDING Invite students to look back over the book. Make sure they understand that it is realistic fiction, not a fantasy. Ask them how they know it is a fictional story instead of a nonfiction book. Have them name the main character and explain what makes him the main character.

RESPONSE OPTIONS

WRITING Ask students to imagine that their parents told them the family would be moving at the end of the school year. Have students write a paragraph discussing how they would feel. Ask whether they would be excited or sad—or both—and why.

SOCIAL STUDIES CONNECTION

Ask students to use the Internet or library to find the population of their city or town. Based on this information, determine whether it is considered a big city, small town, or something in between. Depending on the size, ask students to name a comparable town or city located in your same state.

Skill Work

TEACH/REVIEW VOCABULARY

Write each of the vocabulary words on the chalkboard, and ask students to find them in the reader. To reinforce the contextual meaning of the vocabulary words, ask students how they can tell what each word means by the clues in the surrounding sentence(s).

TARGET SKILL AND STRATEGY

AUTHOR'S PURPOSE Remind students that the *author's purpose* is the reason why he or she wrote the story. An author's purpose can be to inform, entertain, persuade, or express a mood or feeling. After reading, invite students to discuss what they think the author's purpose was in *Bobby's New Apartment*.

PRIOR KNOWLEDGE Invite students to take notes while reading the book. Ask them to make a note whenever the book reminds them of their own lives. Explain that their own experience, as it relates to the story, is called *prior knowledge*. Suggest that they list the page number and then complete this sentence: "This part of the book reminds me of. . . ." or "This character reminds me of. . . ."

ADDITIONAL SKILL INSTRUCTION

REALISM AND FANTASY Remind students that a *realistic story* tells about something that could happen, and a *fantasy* is a story about something that could not happen. Ask students if they think *Bobby's New Apartment* is a realistic story or a fantasy. Then ask students to write two clues from the reader that support their answer. Examples: Bobby is a realistic boy, as described on page 3. The descriptions of the city and building are realistic.

Author's Purpose

- The **author's purpose** is the reason or reasons an author wrote a story.
- An author may have one or more reasons for writing. He or she may want to **inform, persuade, entertain,** or **express** a mood or feeling.

Directions Reread *Bobby's New Apartment* and then answer the following questions.

1. Why do you think the author wrote that "It looked like there were a hundred buttons" in the elevator?

   _____

   _____

2. What did the author write that made you laugh or entertained you?

   _____

   _____

3. Why do you think the author wrote about the basement?

   _____

   _____

4. Why do you think the author wrote that the first time Bobby rode the elevator it made his stomach feel funny?

   _____

   _____

5. Why do you think the author wrote *Bobby's New Apartment*?

   _____

   _____

Name _____

Vocabulary

Directions Read each sentence. Fill in the blank with the word from the word box that fits best.

Check the Words You Know

___cardboard	___feast	___fierce	___flights
___pitcher	___ruined	___stoops	___treasure

1. Instead of walking up twenty-one _____, Bobby took the elevator.

2. The pizza made a perfect _____ for their first night in the apartment.

3. When they came into the apartment, the floors were covered with _____.

4. Bobby thought the doorman had a _____ expression.

5. The painters had been careful that nothing was _____ by their work.

6. The boys found what looked like a key to a _____ while playing on the roof.

7. Bobby's mother brought a _____ of lemonade to drink with the pizza.

Directions Imagine you have been invited to play at the playground on Bobby's roof. Write a paragraph about it using as many vocabulary words as possible.

_____

_____

_____

_____

_____

Symbols, Signs, and Songs of America

SUMMARY This book gives students information about cultural icons of the United States, including Uncle Sam, the bald eagle, and the Stars and Stripes. Students will learn more about the creation, meaning, and importance of these symbols of freedom and how they are used in our society.

LESSON VOCABULARY

crown	liberty
models	symbol
tablet	torch
unforgettable	unveiled

INTRODUCE THE BOOK

INTRODUCE THE TITLE AND AUTHOR Discuss with students the title and the author of *Symbols, Signs, and Songs of America*. Ask students if they recognize any of the cover photographs, and if they know how each one relates to the title.

BUILD BACKGROUND Discuss with students what American signs, symbols, or songs they already know and why each one represents something about America. Ask students why they think a country needs symbols.

PREVIEW/USE TEXT FEATURES Suggest students look at the captions and the subheads in the book. Ask students how they think these elements help organize the book and help them understand the main idea of the book.

READ THE BOOK

SET PURPOSE Have students *set a purpose* for reading *Symbols, Signs, and Songs of America*. Students' curiosity about symbols should guide this purpose.

STRATEGY SUPPORT: QUESTIONING To help students understand how to answer questions, have them write the following headings on a piece of paper: Where I Looked in the Text and What I Knew. As students find answers to questions from Reader Response have them write down how they found the answer to each question.

COMPREHENSION QUESTIONS

PAGE 4 What is the main idea of this page and what are two supporting details? *(The main idea is that America has many symbols. The supporting details are that the flag is one symbol and the bald eagle is another.)*

PAGE 11 Why would the cartoon encourage people to join the armed forces? *(Uncle Sam is pointing and looking directly into your eyes, making it seem as though he is asking you personally to join the armed forces.)*

PAGE 12 What details help you understand why the Statue of Liberty is such an important symbol? *(The statue is a symbol of the friendship between France and America. The crown represents the seven seas and continents of the world, the torch lights the way to America, and the tablet has the date of the Declaration of Independence.)*

PAGE 14 How does the heading give you an idea of what the topic will be about? *(The heading is about our nation's government buildings.)*

REVISIT THE BOOK

READER RESPONSE

1. Fact: The statue was designed by Frederic Bartholdi. Opinion: The Statue of Liberty is one of the United States' most famous symbols.
2. Responses will vary but should include a question.
3. unforgettable, unveiled, *un-* Answers will vary but can include *unlikely* or *unable.* Sentences will vary.
4. Answers will vary but should show some understanding of a battle scene and the inspiring effect of the flag waving.

EXTEND UNDERSTANDING Discuss organizational patterns with students, such as chronological or time order. Explain that signal words give students clues to these patterns. Suggest students brainstorm a list of words that indicate time *(when, then, after that time, first, next, finally)* and list the clue words they find in this book.

RESPONSE OPTIONS

WRITING Ask students to research the turkey and the bald eagle. Then have students imagine they are Benjamin Franklin and write an argument about why the turkey should be our national bird instead of the bald eagle. Suggest students work into their writings the facts they learned as they researched.

SOCIAL STUDIES CONNECTION

Divide students into groups and invite them to form their own country. Ask students to consider what kind of country they want to create and then have them draw a flag for that country, create a symbol, and write lyrics for a short national song. Share with the class.

Skill Work

TEACH/REVIEW VOCABULARY

Review with students the dictionary meaning of each vocabulary word. Then invite students to create clues for the words, following these models: Something that ___; this describes ___; and so on. Let students work in pairs to answer each others' clues.

ELL Suggest students make flashcards, writing a riddle for each vocabulary word on one side and the word on the other. Use the flashcards in class.

TARGET SKILL AND STRATEGY

FACT AND OPINION Remind students that a statement of *fact* is something that can be proven true or false and a statement of *opinion* is something someone thinks or believes. Point out words such as *worst, too much,* and *beautiful* give clues that a sentence is a statement of opinion. Give students ten sentences, half of which are fact and half opinion. Ask students to identify which is which.

QUESTIONING Tell students that a question might have an answer right in the pages of the story. Other times a question will require readers to use their own prior knowledge to figure out what an author means, not just what an author writes. Ask students to read question 1 in Readers Response and identify how they might answer the question.

ADDITIONAL SKILL INSTRUCTION

MAIN IDEA Review with students that the *main idea* is the most important point about a topic. The main idea is sometimes not stated directly, but the details of a selection can give clues to the main idea. Have students read one section of the book and fill in a graphic organizer with the headings: *Topic, Main Ideas,* and *Supporting Details.*

Fact and Opinion

- A statement of **fact** is one that can be proved true or false.
- A statement of **opinion** is a statement of someone's judgment, belief, or way of thinking about something.

Directions Write *F* beside statements of fact and *O* beside statements of opinion.

1. _____ A symbol is something that stands for something else.

2. _____ Betsy Ross enjoyed sewing our nation's first flag.

3. _____ Francis Scott Key was thrilled to see the flag waving over Fort McHenry at dawn.

4. _____ Our nation has many symbolic songs.

5. _____ America's official seal represents war and peace.

6. _____ Uncle Sam is an unforgettable symbol.

7. _____ July 4, 1776 is the date of the Declaration of Independence.

8. _____ Many monuments throughout the country symbolize accomplishments of past leaders.

9–10. Directions Read the statement: *The Liberty Bell is the most important symbol of our country.* Is it a fact or an opinion? Why?

_____

_____

_____

_____

_____

Name _____

Vocabulary

Directions Use five of these vocabulary words to write a story about the signs and symbols of America. Then write definitions for the words you don't use in your story.

Check the Words You Know

___crown   ___liberty   ___models
___symbol   ___tablet   ___torch
___unforgettable   ___unveiled

1. _____

_____

_____

_____

_____

_____

_____

_____

_____

2. _____

3. _____

4. _____

A Pet Bird

SUMMARY This book tells how to care for a pet bird. Birds make wonderful pets, especially if they receive the right kind of care and feeding. This book describes what to do to make your bird happy and healthy.

LESSON VOCABULARY

bows	chilly
foolish	foreign
narrow	perches
recipe	

INTRODUCE THE BOOK

INTRODUCE THE TITLE AND AUTHOR Discuss with students the title and the author of *A Pet Bird*. Ask students what they think the book will be about, based on the title and the pictures and captions in the book.

BUILD BACKGROUND Ask students if any of them have a pet bird. If so, ask them to tell the class what they have to do to care for their bird. Have them share their pets' names. Ask them if their pets are able to speak, and if so, what they can say.

PREVIEW/USE ILLUSTRATIONS Suggest students skim the text and look at the illustrations and captions. Ask the students what clues these elements give them as to what this book might be about.

ELL Ask students whether they have pet birds. If so, have them share the pets' names. Have them share with the class how to say *bird* in their native language.

READ THE BOOK

SET PURPOSE Have students set a purpose for reading *A Pet Bird*. Students' interest and curiosity about pets can guide this purpose. As students read, suggest they take notes that might provide answers to any questions they might have about the subject.

STRATEGY SUPPORT: INFERRING Remind students that *inferring* is combining what they already know with information they read to learn new information. Model using page 12. Say: I know that many animals do not like to be cold. After reading the heading *Keeping Your Pet Bird Warm* I can infer that birds do not like to be cold either.

COMPREHENSION QUESTIONS

PAGE 5 Which birds can be taught how to talk? *(birds of the parrot family—parrots, parakeets, lovebirds, cockatiels, macaws, and conures)*

PAGE 11 Why does a bird need to have grit in its diet? *(Birds do not have teeth to grind their food.)*

PAGE 12 What could happen if a bird is kept in a draft? *(It could get chilly.)*

PAGE 19 If a bird is not acting normally, what should the owner do? *(Call the veterinarian.)*

REVISIT THE BOOK

READER RESPONSE
1. It can get lonely or anxious.
2. Responses will vary but should include an inference.
3. chilly, warm; sentences will vary.
4. Things to Do Before You Bring Your Bird Home: get a cage, make sure the cage has several perches, get toys, get things for the bird to chew on
Things to Do After You Bring Your Bird Home: change water every day, change newspaper every day, give bird a bowl of water to bathe in, give bird grit, give bird a mineral block, keep bird warm and quiet, give bird 10–12 hours of darkness per day

EXTEND UNDERSTANDING Have the students look through the book again and look at all the photographs. Ask the students which bird was their favorite and why. Encourage them to find out more about that bird on the Internet or in the library.

RESPONSE OPTIONS
WRITING Have students imagine that they are going to the pet store to pick out a pet bird. Say: Write about how you decided on a particular bird and what you will name it. Describe your bird in detail.

SOCIAL STUDIES CONNECTION

Time For SOCIAL STUDIES

Have students pick out one of the birds mentioned in the book and research it on the Internet or in the library. What country is the bird native to? What is its native habitat? Have each student report back to the classroom.

Skill Work

TEACH/REVIEW VOCABULARY
Ask students why they think the word *foreign* may be used in a book on birds. Ask them to look at the other vocabulary words and predict their use in a book about keeping birds as pets.

TARGET SKILL AND STRATEGY
CAUSE AND EFFECT Remind students that an *effect* is what happened and a *cause* is why it happened. Have students read pages 12 and 13. What could cause a bird to get chilly? *(cold drafts near the cage)* What could happen to a bird that is left in the sun? *(could become overheated)*

INFERRING Ask students to brainstorm about what they know about birds. Tell students to keep this prior knowledge in mind while they are reading. After reading, ask students to combine their prior knowledge about birds with information from the story to learn something new.

ADDITIONAL SKILL INSTRUCTION
MAIN IDEA Remind students that to summarize means to boil down a story to its *main ideas.* Ask students to take notes as they read, listing the main points and supporting ideas for those main points.

Name _____

Cause and Effect

- A **cause** is why something happened.
- An **effect** is what happened.

Directions Use *A Pet Bird* to fill in each missing cause or effect.

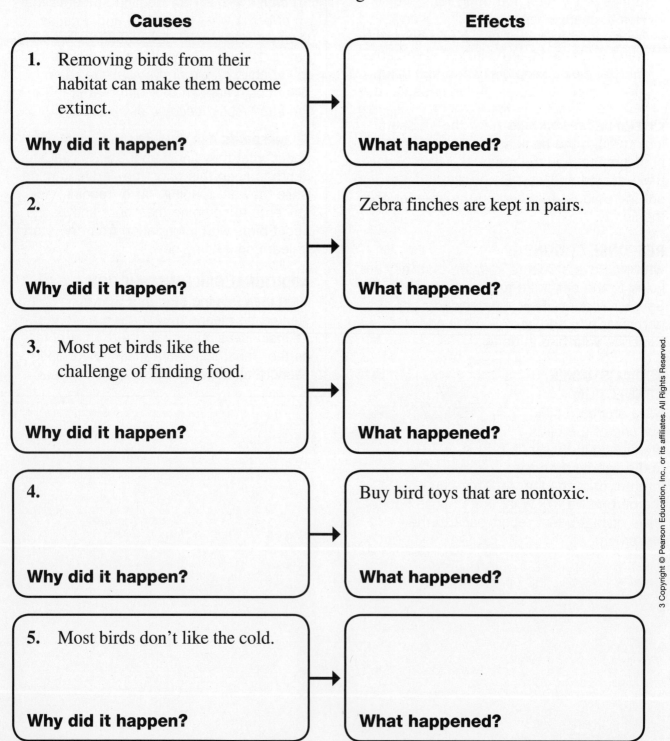

Causes	Effects
1. Removing birds from their habitat can make them become extinct. **Why did it happen?**	**What happened?**
2. **Why did it happen?**	Zebra finches are kept in pairs. **What happened?**
3. Most pet birds like the challenge of finding food. **Why did it happen?**	**What happened?**
4. **Why did it happen?**	Buy bird toys that are nontoxic. **What happened?**
5. Most birds don't like the cold. **Why did it happen?**	**What happened?**

Vocabulary

Directions Fill in the blank with the word from the box that matches the definition.

> ## Check the Words You Know
>
> ___ bows ___ chilly ___ foolish
> ___ foreign ___ narrow ___ perches
> ___ recipe

1. _____ *adj.* from a country other than your own

2. _____ *n.* places to view things from high above

3. _____ *v.* leans forward to show respect

4. _____ *adj.* silly; not wise

5. _____ *n.* instructions for cooking

6. _____ *adj.* having a small width; not very wide

7. _____ *adj.* slightly cold

Directions Write a brief paragraph discussing how to care for a pet bird. Use at least three vocabulary words.

_____

_____

_____

_____

_____

_____

_____

_____

Lily's Adventure Around the World

SUMMARY In this story, a young girl learns about the diversity of expression in Chicago's ethnic neighborhoods. The story supports the lesson concept of freedom of expression.

LESSON VOCABULARY

encourages	expression
local	native
settled	social
support	

INTRODUCE THE BOOK

INTRODUCE THE TITLE AND AUTHOR Discuss with students the title and the author of *Lily's Adventure Around the World*. Also have students look at the picture on the cover. Tell students that social studies is the study of how people live as a group. Ask: How might this story have something to do with social studies?

BUILD BACKGROUND Lead a discussion about how many Americans follow customs that come from other countries. Ask: What are some of the ways groups enjoy their differences? What are some things that all Americans try to do in the same way?

PREVIEW/TAKE A PICTURE WALK As students preview the book, encourage them to look closely at the illustrations and ask what information about the story these illustrations provide. Encourage students to ask "What is happening?" and "Why is it happening?" Have students read the heading on page 20. Explain that *ethnic* means having to do with large groups of people who are identified by their common culture. Ask: What is the purpose of this part of the book?

READ THE BOOK

SET PURPOSE Have students set a purpose for reading *Lily's Adventure Around the World*. Remind students of what they discussed in their Preview. Help students by asking them to complete one of these sentences: I wonder _____. I really want to know about _____.

IMPORTANT IDEAS Explain to students that how the text is displayed can help students find important ideas. Tell students these ideas will help them understand why the author wrote the selection. Tell students to look at page 3 and find the important ideas from each paragraph. Ask: How do these ideas help you understand why the author wrote *Lily's Adventure Around the World*?

COMPREHENSION QUESTIONS

PAGES 5–6 Why do you think Lily's dad wanted to show her Chicago? *(Possible response: He wanted her to feel good about staying there.)*

PAGES 10–11 Why do you think so many Polish immigrants settled in the same area? *(Possible response: They felt comfortable with people who shared the same customs.)*

PAGE 15 Read this statement: *Bobak's had one hundred different kinds of sausage.* Is this a statement of fact or a statement of opinion? Why? *(It is a statement of fact because it can be proved true or false.)*

PAGES 18–19 How is Lily at the beginning of the story different from how she is at the end? *(Possible response: At the beginning she did not like Chicago, but at the end she was happy.)*

REVISIT THE BOOK

READER RESPONSE

1. Possible responses: Pilsen—there were colorful murals everywhere; Archer Park—notices a sign in Polish in the bank's window; Chinatown—everyone was speaking Chinese, but it didn't sound like the same Chinese language.

2. Responses will vary.

3. *il gi:* diary, Korean; *enchilada:* a rolled and filled tortilla, Spanish; *gracias:* thank you, Spanish; *chayote:* cactus, Spanish; *mowimy po polsku:* we speak Polish, Polish; *kielbasa, kiszka, bolszewik:* sausages, Polish; *pagodas:* towers with curving roofs, Chinese; *karate, tai chi:* forms of martial arts and exercises, Chinese

4. Possible responses: No, Lily's family is not unique. Many people are interested in the cultures to be found in the United States.

EXTEND UNDERSTANDING Ask students to think about the neighborhoods in this story. Have them make a Venn diagram to compare and contrast two neighborhoods.

RESPONSE OPTIONS

WRITING Have students write a letter to a pen pal from one of the neighborhoods in the story. They should explain how they express themselves through their family and community traditions.

SOCIAL STUDIES CONNECTION

Have students use an atlas, encyclopedia, or gazetteer to look up facts about one of the countries of origin in the story. Have them summarize and share these facts in small groups.

Skill Work

TEACH/REVIEW VOCABULARY

Distribute cards for each of the vocabulary words. Make additional word cards for *human*, *help*, *born here*, *peopled*, *face*, *cheers*, *nearby*. Reinforce word meaning by asking students to show the vocabulary word that best matches each word card.

ELL Give students vocabulary word cards. Have them sort the cards by the number of syllables in each word.

TARGET SKILL AND STRATEGY

GRAPHIC SOURCES Tell students that graphic sources are chats or diagrams that help students understand what they have read. Invite students use prior knowledge to make a KWL chart. Have them fill in the first section, "What I Know," and the second section, "What I Want to Know." Suggest as students read, they fill in the last section, "What I Learned." Remind students that using a graphic organizer can help them determine the plot and the big idea of the story.

IMPORTANT IDEAS Remind students that *important ideas* are the ideas that will give readers insight into why an author wrote a selection. Model using page 6. Say: Before I read this page, I know that an important idea would include learning about culture because of the story's title. Tell students that these ideas can be presented through headings, illustrations, or description.

ADDITIONAL SKILL INSTRUCTION

COMPARE AND CONTRAST Remind students that a *comparison* tells how two or more things are alike, and that a *contrast* shows how two or more things are different. Encourage them to ask questions such as, *How are Pilsen and Chinatown alike?* and *How is Lily's life different from mine?* as they read this story.

Name _____

Graphic Sources

- **Graphic sources** present information visually and can help you better understand the text.
- Graphic sources include, maps, photographs and captions, time lines, diagrams, graphs, and charts.

Directions Compare and contrast the Polish neighborhood with Chinatown. Use the chart below for your answers.

Polish Neighborhood	Chinatown

Name _____

Vocabulary

Directions Fill in the blank with the word that best completes each sentence.

Check the Words You Know

___encourages	___expression	___local	___native
___settled	___social	___support	

---

1. She doesn't play much with other kids. She is not very _____.

2. Lily shopped at the _____ fish market in her neighborhood.

3. Lily's family moved to many places, then _____ in Chicago.

4. Lily's grandmother _____ her to keep a diary.

5. I was born in Chicago, so that makes me a _____ of Chicago.

6. At first, Lily did not _____ her family's move to Chicago.

7. When Lily saw the colorful neighborhood, she had an excited

   _____ on her face.

Directions Use the words *encourages, social, local,* and *expression* in a short paragraph about your community.

_____

_____

_____

_____

_____

_____

_____

SUMMARY This is a retelling of the traditional tale of *The Three Bears and Goldilocks.* In this version, while the Bear family is letting their oatmeal cool, Goldilocks enters their house. She tries their oatmeal, their chairs, and finally their beds, where she falls asleep. When the Bears return, they find her asleep in Billy Bear's bed. They wake her up, and she goes out to play with Billy Bear. In the end, the Bear family forgives her for disturbing their house.

LESSON VOCABULARY

crystal	disappeared
discovery	goal
journey	joyful
scoop	unaware

INTRODUCE THE BOOK

INTRODUCE THE TITLE AND AUTHOR Discuss with students the title and the author of *The Three Bears and Goldilocks.* What do the title and the cover art suggest the story will be about?

BUILD BACKGROUND Ask students if they know the story of *The Three Bears and Goldilocks.* Have them tell the story in their own words. What are the things that happen to Goldilocks in the story, and in what order do they happen?

PREVIEW/USE ILLUSTRATIONS Have the students look through the illustrations in the book. Do the illustrations seem to tell the story of Goldilocks in the same way that students remember the story?

ELL Have each student tell the story of Goldilocks, if they know it, or another fairy tale from a country they may have visited or lived in.

READ THE BOOK

SET PURPOSE Have students set a purpose for reading *The Three Bears and Goldilocks.* They could trace Goldilocks's actions or the sequence of events in the story.

STRATEGY SUPPORT: STORY STRUCTURE Share with students that story structure is the way a story is organized. Explain that this story is organized chronologically, or in the order in which the events happen. Ask students to make a flowchart for *The Three Bears and Goldilocks.* Tell students that as they read, they should put events in the order they happen and include all important events. Remind students that identifying the structure of a story can help them recognize causes and effects.

COMPREHENSION QUESTIONS

PAGE 4 Why was Billy Bear lonely? *(He lived in the forest far from his friends in town.)*

PAGE 5 What was special about Mom Bear's chair? *(It was covered in soft green velvet.)*

PAGE 9 What sort of crystal animal does Goldilocks break? *(a bunny)*

PAGE 17 What does Goldilocks do when the Bears find her in Billy's bed? *(She runs out of the house.)*

PAGE 17 Why does Mom Bear say that Goldilocks acts mean? *(She says she acts mean because she is lonely.)*

PAGE 18 Does Billy Bear stay angry at Goldilocks? *(No, he forgives her.)*

REVISIT THE BOOK

READER RESPONSE

1. Possible responses: Problem: Dad Bear is angry because of the damage done to the house. Beginning: The Bear Family goes out for a walk while their oatmeal cools. Middle: Goldilocks enters their house, eats their oatmeal, breaks a chair, and goes to sleep in Billy's bed. End: The Bears return home. Solution: They forgive Goldilocks.
2. Responses will vary but should show understanding of story structure.
3. Possible responses: Goldilocks discovers that she is in Billy Bear's house, that she's too heavy for Billy Bear's chair, and that Billy Bear's bed is just right for her. The Bears learn that someone has broken into their house, that a crystal animal and a chair have been broken, and that Goldilocks is sleeping in Billy Bear's bed.
4. Possible response: Goldilocks is selfish, while Billy Bear is forgiving. Responses will vary.

EXTEND UNDERSTANDING Have students think about what the big idea of the story is. What does the story tell us about respecting other people's homes and possessions? What details in the book support that idea?

RESPONSE OPTIONS

WRITING Have students write about a time when they were selfish and did something they regretted but were forgiven. Ask: How did it feel to be forgiven? Did you feel you learned something through that experience? What did you learn?

SCIENCE CONNECTION

Have students research as much as they can to find out about bears. Assign each group of students a different type of bear, such as a brown bear, black bear, polar bear, or grizzly bear. Have each student draw a picture of the group's bear. Once groups have gathered all their information, have them share it with the class.

Skill Work

TEACH/REVIEW VOCABULARY

Encourage student pairs to find the vocabulary words in the text. Have them define the words and then work together to write a sentence for each word.

ELL Ask students to skim the story and write down any unfamiliar words. Suggest that they look the words up in a dictionary and write the meanings in their notebooks.

TARGET SKILL AND STRATEGY

PLOT AND THEME Remind students that the *plot* is the sequence of events that take a story from the beginning to the middle to the end. Also, remind students that stories usually have one big idea or *theme*. Discuss with students what they think the theme is of familiar stories such as *The Tortoise and the Hare (slow and steady wins the race)*. Have them tell the plot of the story by recalling the events in sequence.

STORY STRUCTURE Tell students that they are studying the sequence of the story. Ask students to look at the beginning, middle, and end as they read. Suggest that students fill out graphic organizers as they read.

ADDITIONAL SKILL INSTRUCTION

CHARACTER Remind students that a *character* is a person or animal who takes part in the events of a story. As students read this story, have them try to decide what kind of character Goldilocks is. What is she like, and how do we find this out?

Plot and Theme

- The **plot** is an organized pattern of events.
- The **theme** is the "big idea" of a story.

Directions Fill in the table below, which will guide you through a summary of the plot and end with your naming the theme of *The Three Bears and Goldilocks*.

Title _____

This story is about _____

_____
(name the characters)

This story takes place _____

_____
(where and when)

The action begins when _____

_____

Then, _____

_____

Next, _____

_____

After that, _____

_____

_____

The story ends when _____

_____

Theme: _____

_____

Vocabulary

Directions Fill in the blank with the word from the box that fits best.

Check the Words You Know

___crystal	___disappeared	___discovery	___goal
___journey	___joyful	___scoop	___unaware

1. Mom Bear made breakfast with one large _____ of oatmeal.

2. Goldilocks _____ from the Bears' house in a rush.

3. Goldilocks did not knock the _____ vase off the shelf.

4. The thought of oatmeal for breakfast made Papa Bear feel _____.

5. The Bears were _____ that Goldilocks was upstairs sleeping.

6. The _____ of the Bears' walk was to let the oatmeal cool.

7. The Bears made a big _____ when they returned home.

8. Goldilocks will be more careful on her next _____.

Directions Write a brief paragraph discussing Goldilocks's visit to the Bears' house, using as many vocabulary words as possible.

_____

_____

_____

_____

_____

_____

_____

_____

Sweet Freedom!

SUMMARY This book describes the inventive and remarkable ways three American slaves managed to escape to freedom. Ellen and William Craft used imagination and disguises to travel North together. Henry Brown put himself into a box and mailed the box to freedom.

LESSON VOCABULARY

aqueducts	content
crouched	guidance
honor	pillar
thermal	

INTRODUCE THE BOOK

INTRODUCE THE TITLE AND AUTHOR Discuss the title and author of *Sweet Freedom!* Ask students what they think is happening in the illustration on the cover.

BUILD BACKGROUND Briefly explain to students some facts about slavery in the United States. In the early years of our country, many white people owned slaves who worked for them, both in the fields and in their homes. Most of these people lived in the southern part of the United States. The slaves were people brought from Africa. Slavery was abolished after the Civil War and the presidency of Abraham Lincoln.

PREVIEW/USE TEXT FEATURES Ask students to preview the book by paging through it and looking at the illustrations and headings. Draw attention to the glossary on page 20 and invite volunteers to tell how they might use it.

READ THE BOOK

SET PURPOSE Ask students to set one or more purposes for reading, based on what they found when they previewed the book.

STRATEGY SUPPORT: INFERRING Tell students that good readers often "read between the lines" to figure out something that is not directly stated. Students can combine what they read with what they already know to infer a lesson or to interpret what they have read.

COMPREHENSION QUESTIONS

PAGE 5 What one thing about Ellen Craft made it possible for her and her husband to make their daring escape? *(She was very light-skinned and was able to "pass" as a white person.)*

PAGE 6 How did Ellen disguise the fact that she could not read and write? *(She bandaged her arm to make it appear injured so it could be an excuse for not using it to write.)*

PAGES 13–15 Why do you think Henry Brown had the nickname "Box"? *(because he achieved his freedom by mailing himself in a big box to Philadelphia)*

PAGE 19 How are the stories of the Crafts and Brown connected to the title of the book? *(They fought so hard to gain their freedom from slavery that it must have seemed very sweet to them.)*

REVISIT THE BOOK

READER RESPONSE

1. Responses will vary, but may include the generalization that some slaves went to great lengths to gain their freedom. Supporting facts may include: The Crafts used disguise and trickery to get themselves to the north where slavery was outlawed. Henry Brown went through a difficult trip inside a box to get there.

2. Responses will vary, but students may infer that life in the south included slavery, and that people in the north did not allow slavery and worked to abolish it.

3. The word *content* is on page 9, *guidance* 15, and *honored* 12. Sentences will vary, but make sure students use the word *content* in its meaning of "satisfied" and not in its meaning of "things inside."

4. Responses will vary, but make sure students can defend their choice with elements of the story.

ELL Point out to students that the word *content* has two pronunciations, each with its own meaning and use in a sentence. Provide the following sentences orally to show them the distinction: *We were content with our performance in the game. Check the contents of the box.*

EXTEND UNDERSTANDING You may want to discuss with students the fact that African-American people are descended from the slaves who were brought here from Africa many years ago.

RESPONSE OPTIONS

DRAMA Divide students into two groups. Let each team act out either the story of the Crafts or of "Box" Brown and their escapes from slavery.

SOCIAL STUDIES CONNECTION

Time For SOCIAL STUDIES

Challenge students to do some research about the Underground Railroad and/or about Harriet Tubman, Sojourner Truth, and other well-known heroes of escape from slavery.

Skill Work

TEACH/REVIEW VOCABULARY

Students have already written their own sentences containing the vocabulary words *content, guidance,* and *honor*. Ask them to do so with the remaining vocabulary words. Challenge them to try to make their sentences not about the stories in the book.

TARGET SKILL AND STRATEGY

GENERALIZE Recall with students that a broad statement that covers many different ideas is a *generalization*. Provide several examples, such as *This week we have had a lot of rainy weather* or *It often snows here in December*. Remind students that generalizations must be supported by observable facts or statements. Both generalizations above, for example, might be supported by personal observations.

INFERRING Remind students that they can put together what they already know with what they read to learn something new, just as they did when they considered something about life in the United States in the early 1800s.

ADDITIONAL SKILL INSTRUCTION

PLOT AND THEME Review with students that the *plot* of a story is what happens in the beginning, middle, and end of the story. The *theme* is a story's main idea or central meaning. Ask volunteers to briefly tell the plot of each of the stories in *Sweet Freedom!* and then to explain what they think the main idea of both stories together might be.

Generalize

- A **generalization** is a broad statement that applies to many examples.
- Sometimes a generalization is signaled by a clue word such as *all, most, many, never, usually,* or *generally.*
- A generalization should be supported by facts and be reasonable.

Directions Think about the people you read about in *Sweet Freedom!* Write facts and statements about them in the boxes below. Then use those facts to make a generalization about the people.

Ellen and William Craft: Escape to Freedom

1. **Facts and statements about Ellen and William Craft**

_____

_____

_____

2. **Generalization about Ellen and William Craft**

_____

_____

_____

Henry "Box" Brown: Mailed to Freedom

3. **Facts and statements about Henry Brown**

_____

_____

_____

4. **Generalization about Henry "Box" Brown**

_____

_____

_____

Vocabulary

Directions Use each vocabulary word in a sentence as directed.

Check the Words You Know

___aqueducts   ___content   ___crouched
___guidance   ___honor   ___pillar
___thermal

1. Use the word *aqueducts* in a sentence about ancient Greeks.

_____

2. Write a sentence that tells about something that makes you feel *content*.

_____

3. Write a sentence about an animal that includes the word *crouched*.

_____

4. Use the word *guidance* in a sentence about someone who helped you.

_____

5. Write a sentence about someone who received an *honor*.

_____

6. Use the word *pillar* in a sentence about a building.

_____

7. Use the word *thermal* in a sentence about a shirt or jacket.

_____

Story Prediction from Previewing

Title _____

Read the title and look at the pictures in the story.
What do you think a problem in the story might be?

I think a problem might be _____

_____

_____

After reading _____ ,
draw a picture of one of the problems in the story.

Story Prediction from Vocabulary

Title and Vocabulary Words

Read the title and the vocabulary words.
What do you think this story might be about?

I think this story might be about _____

_____

_____

After reading _____ ,
draw a picture that shows what the story is about.

KWL Chart

Topic _____

What We **K**now	What We **W**ant to Know	What We **L**earned

Vocabulary Frame

Word

Association or Symbol

Predicted definition: _____

_____

One good sentence:

_____

_____

_____

Verified definition: _____

_____

_____

Another good sentence:

_____

_____

_____

Story Predictions Chart

Title _____

What might happen?	What clues do I have?	What did happen?

Story Sequence A

Title _____

Beginning

Middle

End

Story Sequence B

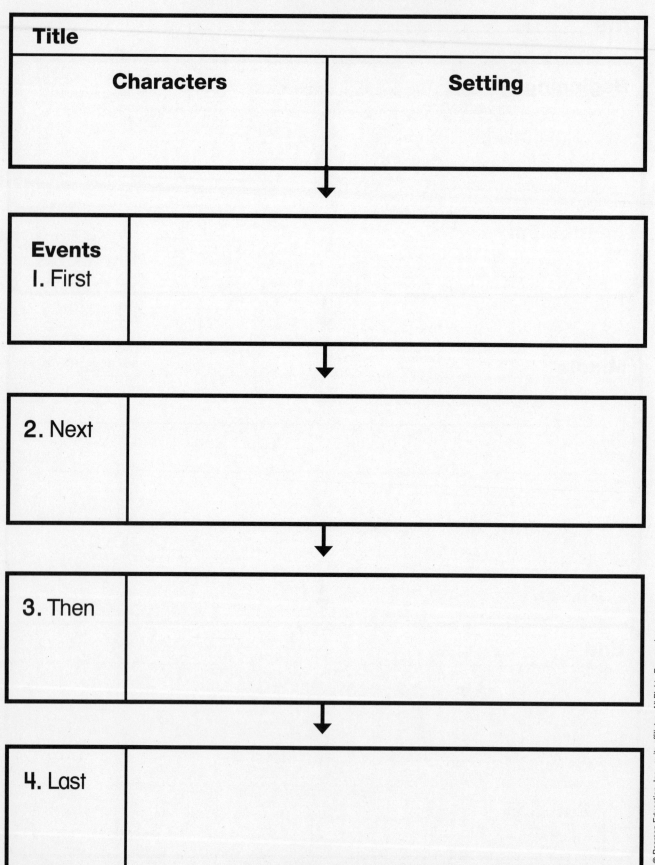

Title	
Characters	**Setting**

Events 1. First	

2. Next	

3. Then	

4. Last	

Story Sequence C

Title

Characters

Problem

Events

_____

_____

_____

_____

_____

_____

_____

_____

Solution

Question the Author

Title _____

Author _____ **Page** _____

1. What does the author tell you?	
2. Why do you think the author tells you that?	
3. Does the author say it clearly?	
4. What would make it clearer?	
5. How would you say it instead?	

Story Comparison

Title A _____

Title B _____

Characters

Setting

Events

Characters

Setting

Events

Web

Main Idea

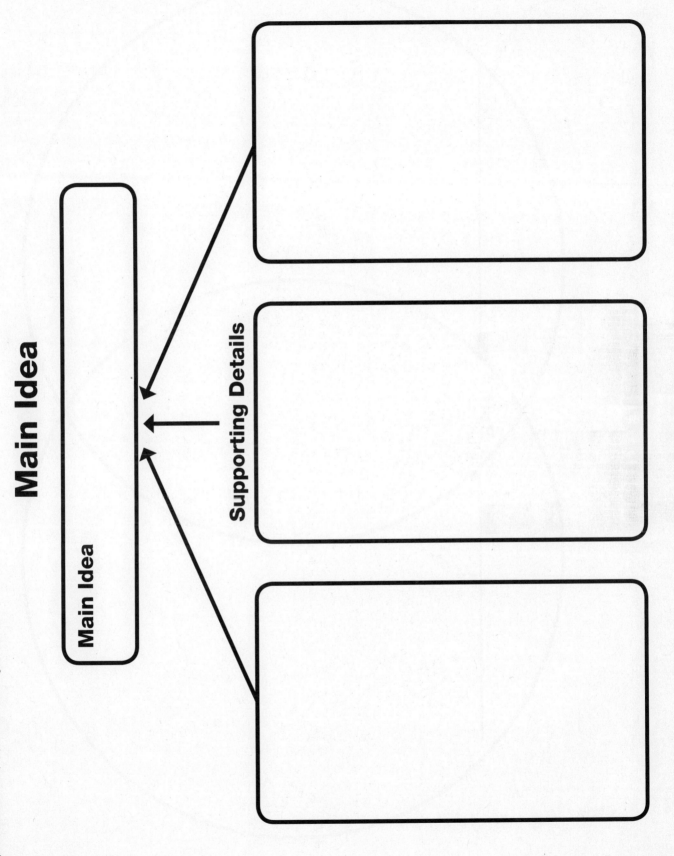

Main Idea

Supporting Details

Venn Diagram

Both

Compare and Contrast

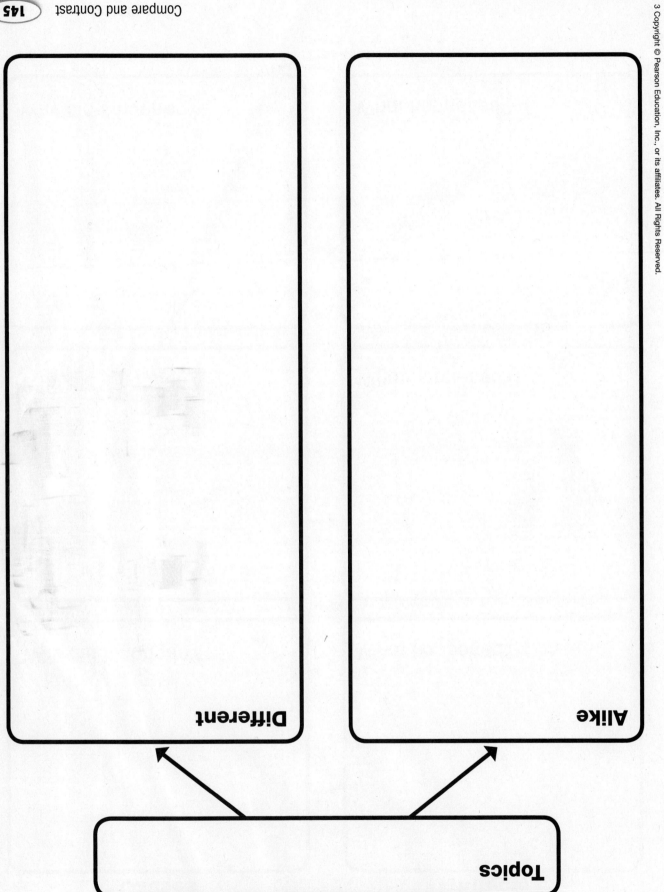

Topics

Alike

Different

Cause and Effect

Causes

Effects

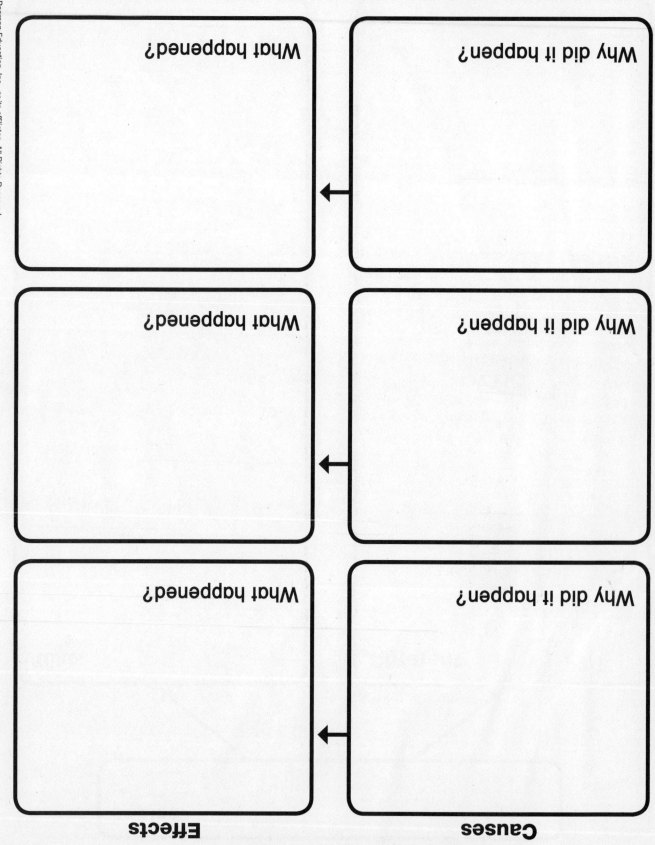

Why did it happen?

What happened?

Why did it happen?

What happened?

Why did it happen?

What happened?

Problem and Solution

Problem

Attempts to Solve the Problem

Solution

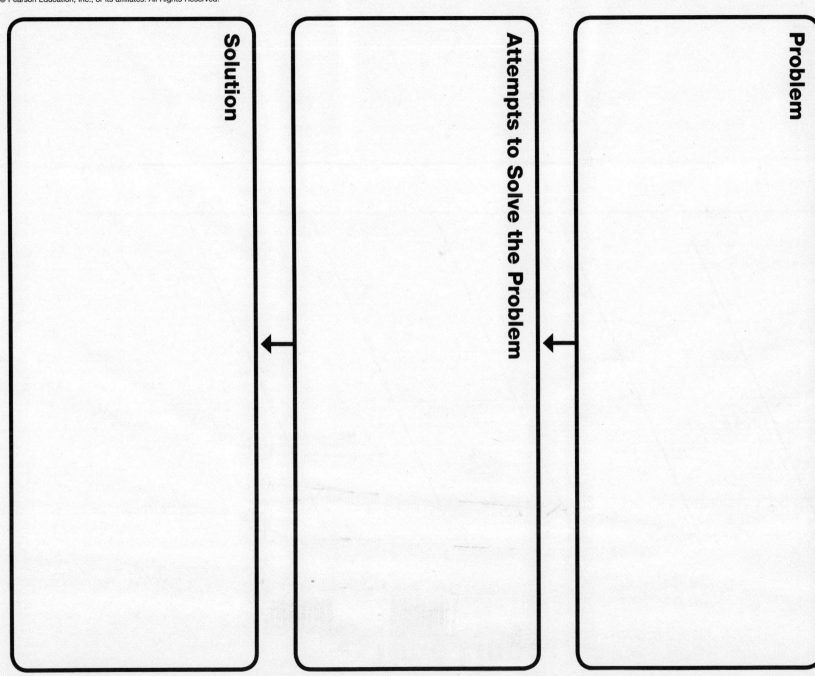

Time Line

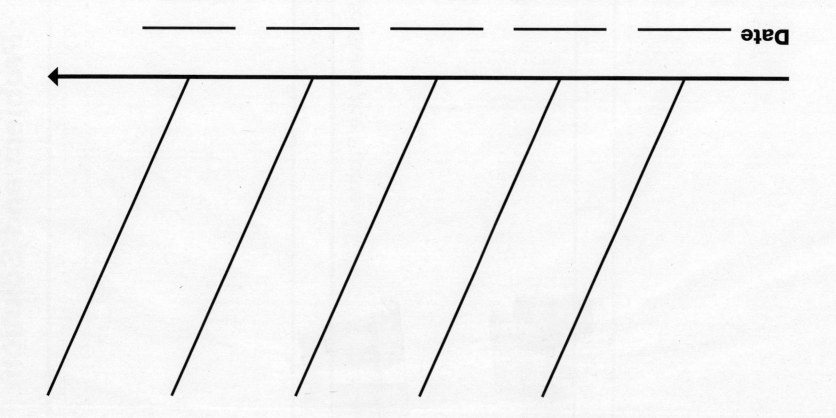

Date

Steps in a Process

Process _____

Step 1

Step 2

Step 3

Three-Column Chart

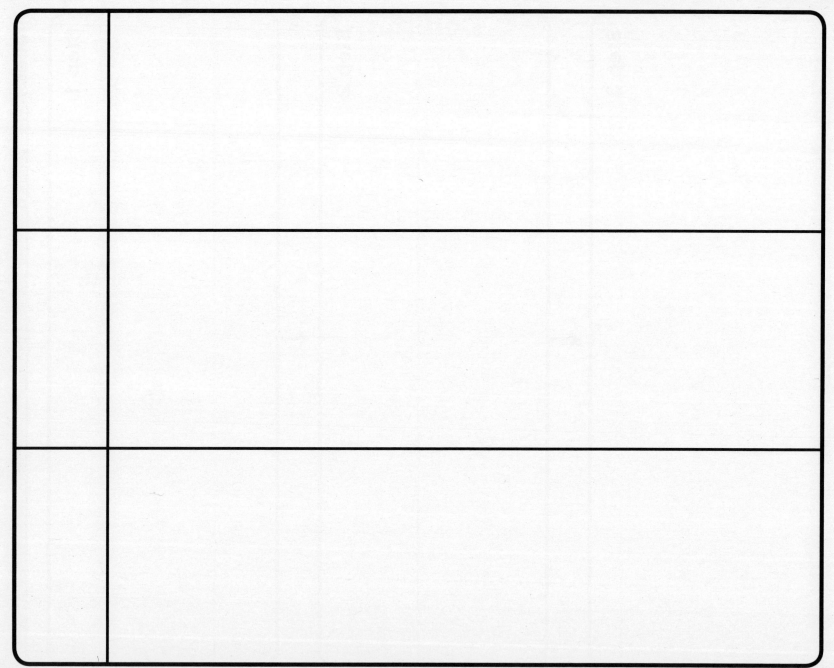

Four-Column Chart

Four-Column Graph

Title _____

Answer Key

Leveled Reader Practice Pages

Camping with Aunt Julie p. 14
CHARACTER AND SETTING

1. friendly and enjoys spending time with her nephew.
2. a caring and generous aunt who wants to share experiences with her nephew.
3. prepared and enthusiastic about their camping trip.
4. Paragraphs will vary but should include descriptions of the characters and setting.

Camping with Aunt Julie p. 15 Vocabulary

1. blew
2. battery
3. fuel
4. plug, battery
5. vision
6. term
7. bat
8. blew

9–12. Sentences will vary but should show students' understanding of vocabulary words.

Let's Make a Trade! p. 18
SEQUENCE

1. People decide what skills or goods they have to offer in trade for skills and goods that they want. People meet and agree to trade, or bargain for a trade, or not have a trade at all.
2. Native Americans bartered animal furs for the cloth, thread, and tools the colonists had.
3. The students display their items to trade. They decide what they want to barter for. Students find items to trade or keep their own items.
4. The theater offered free office space to a local radio station that needed it in exchange for free advertising.
5. Possible responses: Mr. Smith could offer his business knowledge to help Mr. Jones in his carpentry business in exchange for Mr. Jones's building him a table. The Jones daughter could tutor the Smith daughters in math in exchange for a sports card.

Let's Make a Trade! p. 19 Vocabulary

1. carpenter
2. knowledge
3. marketplace
4. plenty
5. straying
6. thread
7. carpetmaker
8. merchant
9. marketplace
10. plenty
11. thread
12. merchant

13–16. Definitions will vary but should show an understanding of the vocabulary words.

Ice Fishing in the Artic p. 22
SEQUENCE

Possible responses:

1–3. First, she set a goal. Next, she decided how much time she had to save money. Then, she decided how much to save each week.

4–6. First, Darla decided that she wanted to save money to go on the ice-fishing trip. Then, Darla made a savings plan. Finally, Darla opened a savings account.

Ice Fishing in the Artic p. 23 Vocabulary

1. willow
2. splendid
3. twitch
4. parka
5. yanked
6. gear

8–9. Sentences will vary but should show an understanding of the vocabulary words.

The Shopping Trip p. 26
COMPARE AND CONTRAST

Possible responses:

1. slept late on Saturday
2. relaxed and did fun activities
3. everyone is tired
4. hardly any food in the refrigerator

The Shopping Trip p. 27 Vocabulary

1. spoiled
2. laundry
3. store
4. traded
5. variety
6. section, store
7. shelves
8. thousands

9–10. Sentences will vary but should show an understanding of the vocabulary words.

The Market Adventure p. 30
AUTHOR'S PURPOSE
1. To express a mood or feeling.
2. To entertain
3. To entertain
4. Responses will vary but should show a clear purpose for writing.

The Market Adventure p. 31
1. errands, unwrapped
2. excitedly
3. bundles
4. steady, dangerously

Paragraphs will vary but should show an understanding of the vocabulary words.

These Birds Can't Fly! p. 34
MAIN IDEA AND DETAILS
Possible responses:
1. flightless birds
2. Flightless birds differ from flying birds in many ways.
3. The bones of flightless birds are heavier than those of flying birds.
4. Flightless birds' feathers are also different than those of flying birds.
5. A flightless bird's breastbone has no flight muscles attached to it like flying birds.

These Birds Can't Fly! p. 35 Vocabulary
1. hugs, snuggles
2. paddles, fins
3. chilly, icy
4. produce, cause
5. strikes, hits
6. dress, groom
7. nestles, holds

Paragraphs will vary but should show an understanding of the vocabulary words.

Iguana Takes a Ride p. 38
COMPARE AND CONTRAST
Possible responses:
1–2. The boatman offered a ride for five dollars. Boatman is safe.
3–4. Crocodile is not safe. Crocodile offered a free ride.
5. Responses will vary but should include details from the story.

Iguana Takes a Ride p. 39 Vocabulary
1. lovable, cute
2. sympathetic, understanding
3. just so, precisely
4. tropical lizard, animal with tail
5. composed, full-grown
6. speak about, say quickly
7. prizes, awards

The Last Minute p. 42
DRAW CONCLUSIONS
Possible responses:
Facts: Katy did not start her book because she had to clean her room; Pam told Katy she leaves things until the last minute.
Conclusion: Katy will have to finish her book report in one day.

The Last Minute p. 43 Vocabulary
1. insects, Monarchs
2. group, set
3. huge, giant
4. separated, sprinkled
5. ties, shoestrings
6. try, strive

Paragraphs will vary but should show an understanding of the vocabulary words.

Our Garden p. 46
AUTHOR'S PURPOSE
Possible responses:
1. to show how much work is involved
2. to show that people working together can do great things
3. The author tells what they can accomplish by working together.
4. the heartwarming way the author shows how people improve their community
5. by trying to convince people that good things come from working together

Our Garden p. 47 Vocabulary
1. wealth
2. lazy
3. bottom
4. cheat
5. lazy
6. crops
7. clever
8. partners

Sentences will vary but should show an understanding of the vocabulary words.

Bills and Beaks p. 50
MAIN IDEA AND DETAILS
Possible responses:
1. birds' bills
2. the uses for birds' bills
3. Birds pick up nest materials with their bills.
4. Birds clean themselves with their bills.
5. The most important use for a bird's bill is to eat.

Bills and Beaks p. 51 Vocabulary
1. bill
2. goo
3. twigs
4. platform
5. material
6. hunters
7. bill
8. tons
9. goo
10. twigs

Sentences will vary but should show an understanding of the vocabulary words.

Leveled Reader Practice Pages

In the Fields p. 54
DRAW CONCLUSIONS

Possible responses:
1. lived in poor conditions; paid very little
2. We would be upset because conditions were not fair.
3. The workers went on strike to fight for better pay and living conditions.

In the Fields p. 55 Vocabulary
1. artificial
2. area
3. preservative
4. Grapevines
5. Raisins
6. raise
7. proof
   Sentences will vary.

The Thunder and Lightning Men p. 58
CHARACTERS, SETTING, AND PLOT

1. the man and the chief
2. in the sky
3. hundreds years ago
4. Beginning: A man is carried away to the village of thunders where the thunder and lightning men live.
   Middle: The man becomes a thunder and lightning man and enjoys himself.
   End: The man tells the chief of the thunder and lightning men that he wants to go home, so the chief sends him home.

The Thunder and Lightning Men
p. 59 Vocabulary
1. antlers, on the deer's head
2. overhead, up high
3. poked, my finger into his tummy
4. narrator, who explained what was happening
5. languages, speaks, English
6. imagined, pictures in my head, what it would be like
7–8. Sentences will vary but should show an understanding of the vocabulary words.

Meet the Stars p. 62
GRAPHIC SOURCES

1. First, Arnie moved to a new town, Benton, which he did not like.
2. Next, Arnie was invited to Meet the Stars.
3. Then, Arnie went to Ms. Williston house to Meet the Stars and learned how Benton is fun.
4. Last, Arnie made a new friend and started to enjoy living in Benton

Meet the Stars p. 63 Vocabulary
1. gigantic
2. shine
3. dim
4. patterns
5. temperature
6. ladle
7. gas
   Sentences will vary.

What a Day! p. 66
GENERALIZE

Possible responses:
Generalization: Most of the dogs are attached to Dana.
Details 1–3: Many dogs race to greet Dana; Shy Elvis sits on Dana's lap; Dana spends time with each dog.

What a Day! p. 67 Vocabulary
1. melody
2. channel
3. surrounded
4. chipped
5. blizzard
6. anxiously
7. symphony
8. supplies
9. bay
10. Sentences will vary but should show an understanding of the vocabulary words.

Desert Life p. 70
CAUSE AND EFFECT

1. they adapt, Plants and animals survive in the desert
2. they can go out to find food at night, Desert kangaroo rats sleep during the hot desert days
3. there is little water in the desert, cactus plants store water
4. the armadillo lizard becomes frightened, it rolls itself up
5. the Gila monster hunts at night, it can't be seen very well
6. ability to store water, cesert tortoises can go for years without drinking
7. it gets too hot, cactus wrens look for food in shady areas
8. rain, dramatic changes in the desert

Desert Life p. 71 Vocabulary
1. unseen
2. incredible
3. search
4. waterless
5. survivors
6. topic
7. sting
8. noble
9. lofty

A Trip p. 74
GENERALIZE
Possible responses:
1. invented basketball
2. The Basketball Hall of Fame is named after him.
3. in Springfield, Massachusetts
4. building is shaped like a giant basketball
5. more than seven feet tall
6. made 25,000 points in his lifetime of NBA play
7. played in the Olympics
8. first female to play in a men's professional league

Generalization: Many special basketball players are included in the Hall of Fame named for the inventor of basketball.

A Trip p. 75 Vocabulary
Possible answers:
1. I watch some sports on TV with my dad.
2. You throw a basketball into a hoop for points.
3. Math is one subject we study in school.
4. Our team was terrible so we lost the game.
5. We thought my aunt had a disease called arthritis.
6. Sponge Bob Square Pants is a popular show.
7. When it is really cold, the lakes freeze.
8. Magic Johnson could guard players taller than he was.

Measuring the Earth p. 78
GRAPHIC SOURCES
1. the costal areas
2. Gypsum is a soft mineral.
3. corundum and diamond
4. the bar graph should show the following information:
   Mount St. Helen 8,365 feet
   Pike's Peak 14,115 feet
   Mt. Everest 29,035 feet

Measuring the Earth p. 79 Vocabulary
1. waterfalls
2. deserts
3. peak
4. tides
5. outrun
6. erupted
7. deserts, tides, waterfalls
8. erupted, outrun
9. tides, waterfalls
10. average, depth
11. tides, waterfalls

Fun with Hobbies and Science! p. 82
FACT AND OPINION
1. Fact
2. Opinion
3. Opinion
4. Fact
5. Fact
6–8. Possible responses: Facts: There are many popular science hobbies out there; If you love animals, you can help take care of them; What you learn about animals now, may help you become a veterinarian in the future; A veterinarian is a doctor who takes care of animals. Opinions: Caring for animals can be an interesting hobby; Veterinarians can have tough jobs.

Fun with Hobbies and Science!
p. 83 Vocabulary
Possible responses:
1. I like to work on my hobbies after I complete my chores.
2. Every butterfly is labeled in my collection.
3. I have a workbench in the attic to use for my hobbies.
4. Collecting stamps is an interesting hobby.
5. My hobby is playing darts, and I have my own dart board.
6. I enjoy knitting and selling scarves to my costumers.
7. In my spare time, I like to look at the stars.
8. chores, customers, spare, stamps
9. attic, board, customers, label
10. chores, hobby, label, spare
11. attic, binoculars, spare, telescope

Great Women in U.S. History p. 86
FACT AND OPINION
Possible responses:
1. In 1932, Babe went to the Olympic Games in Los Angeles.
2. online; in a biographical encyclopedia
3. Her memory and courage will live forever.
4. the author's belief, and it cannot be proved true of false
5. She died at a young age of cancer, but her memory and courage will live forever. The first part is a statement of fact because it can be checked. The second part is the author's opinion about Babe's memory.

Great Women in U.S. History p. 87 Vocabulary

1. stirred
2. celebrate
3. medal
4. continued
5. strokes
6. drowned
7. current

8–9. Responses will vary but should show an understanding of the vocabulary words.

Buddy Ran Away p. 90
🎯 **CAUSE AND EFFECT**

1. The rabbit was startled.
2. The rabbit ran out of the grass.
3. Buddy chased the rabbit.
4. Buddy got lost.
5. Sam left a scent trail.

Buddy Ran Away p. 91 Vocabulary
Make sure students find all the vocabulary words within the word search.
1–4. Sentences will vary but should show an understanding of the vocabulary words.

Cowboy Slim's Dude Ranch p. 94
🎯 **COMPARE AND CONTRAST**

Possible responses: Life on a Dude Ranch: has horses and cows; house is by a large field Both: places where people live
Life at Home: smaller yard; have dogs and cats
1–2. Responses will vary but should show understanding of comparing and contrasting.

Cowboy Slim's Dude Ranch p. 95 Vocabulary

1. rhythm
2. graceful
3. handkerchief
4. festival
5. pace
6. cotton
7. snug
8. pale

Celebrate Around the World p. 98
🎯 **MAIN IDEA AND DETAILS**

1. The Festival of Lights, or Hanukkah
2–3. Possible answers: The Festival of Lights, or Hanukkah lasts 8 days. Hanukkah is celebrated by Jewish people.
4. Families coming together for the holidays.
5–6. Possible responses: Children's Day is celebrated in Japan on May 5. The fish stands for courage and strength

Celebrate Around the World p. 99 Vocabulary

1. circus
2. bouquets
3. difficult
4. soar
5. pier
6. swallow
7. nibbling

Paragraphs will vary but should show an understanding of the vocabulary words.

Leveled Reader Practice Pages

Joanie's House Becomes a Home p. 102
🎯 **SEQUENCE**

1. d
2. c
3. b
4. e
5. a

Joanie's House Becomes a Home
p. 103 Vocabulary

1. a place where airplanes take off and land
2. a room below ground in a house
3. eager to find out about something
4. very tasty
5. told about, explained
6. an expression of good wishes when saying good-bye
7. missing friends and family
8. thoughts of what happened in the past
9. drops of water falling from clouds
10–11. Responses will vary but should show an understanding of the vocabulary words.

Kapuapua's Magic Shell p. 106
🎯 **DRAW CONCLUSIONS**

Possible responses:
Facts: Kapuapua has a plan. The villagers don't like strangers.
Conclusion: Everyone can be fooled sometimes.

Kapuapua's Magic Shell p. 107 Vocabulary

1. batch
2. mixture
3. ingredients
4. bakery
5. braided
6. boils
7. dough

Paragraphs will vary but should show an understanding of the vocabulary words.

Bobby's New Apartment p. 110
🎯 **AUTHOR'S PURPOSE**

Possible responses:

1. to show that it was a big building
2. when Bobby wondered if people talk in elevators
3. to inform the reader how the trash was taken care of
4. to show Bobby was scared
5. to inform the reader about apartment living

Bobby's New Apartment p. 111 Vocabulary

1. flights
2. feast
3. cardboard
4. fierce
5. ruined
6. treasure
7. pitcher

Paragraphs will vary but should show an understanding of the vocabulary words.

Symbols, Signs, and Songs of America p. 114

FACT AND OPINION

1. F
2. O
3. O
4. F
5. F
6. O
7. F
8. F
9–10. Opinion. This statement contains a feeling or belief.

Symbols, Signs, and Songs of America

p. 115 Vocabulary
1–4. Responses will vary but should show an understanding of the vocabulary words.

A Pet Bird p. 118

CAUSE AND EFFECT

1. In the United States it is illegal to import birds from many countries.
2. Zebra finches don't like to be lonely.
3. Place interesting treats in different parts of your bird's cage.
4. Birds like to chew on their toys.
5. Make sure there are no cold drafts near the cage.

A Pet Bird p. 119 Vocabulary

1. foreign
2. perches
3. bows
4. foolish
5. recipe
6. narrow
7. chilly

Paragraphs will vary but should show an understanding of the vocabulary words.

Lily's Adventure Around the World p. 122

GRAPHIC SOURCES

Possible responses: Polish neighborhood: Polish immigrants, South Pulaski Avenue, Polish writing in windows, people speaking Polish, Chinatown: Karate outfits, buildings with traditional Chinese architecture, people speaking Chinese, Chinese immigrants.

Lily's Adventure Around the World

p. 123 Vocabulary
1. social
2. local
3. settled
4. encourages
5. native
6. support
7. expression

Paragraphs will vary but should show an understanding of the vocabulary words.

The Three Bears and Goldilocks p. 126

PLOT AND THEME

Possible responses:

Title: The Three Bears and Goldilocks
About: Goldilocks, Dad Bear, Mom Bear, and Billy Bear
Takes place: in the house of the Bear family
Begins: Mom Bear makes oatmeal that is too hot to eat. The family goes for a walk while it cools.
Then: Goldilocks wanders by their house. She goes inside to taste the oatmeal.
Next: She tastes the oatmeal, breaks their chairs and a crystal animal, and falls asleep in Billy Bear's bed.
After that: the Bears return to find the things that Goldilocks broke. They also find her asleep in Billy Bear's bed. She wakes up, says she is sorry and runs off.
Ends: Billy Bear stops her and says he forgives her.
Theme: It is best to respect the property of others.

The Three Bears and Goldilocks

p. 127 Vocabulary
1. scoop
2. disappeared
3. crystal
4. joyful
5. unaware
6. goal
7. discovery
8. journey

Paragraphs will vary but should show an understanding of the vocabulary words.

Sweet Freedom! p. 130

GENERALIZE

Possible responses:
1. Ellen pretended to be a white man with an injured arm while they made their daring escape.
2. They were very eager to escape from slavery, and they worked hard to free themselves and lead the antislavery movement.
3. Henry mailed himself in a box from the South to the North.
4. Henry was so determined to get his freedom from slavery that he had himself mailed north where slavery was illegal.

Sweet Freedom! p. 131 Vocabulary

Possible responses:
1. The ancient Greeks built aqueducts to carry water from place to place.
2. I'm content when we win all our games.
3. The cat crouched when it was ready to pounce.
4. The gym teacher gave us guidance about how to play the game.
5. Jamie got an honor because of his good grades.
6. The bank downtown has big pillars in front.
7. My plaid jacket has a thermal lining.